The Christian Vocation of Forgiveness

The Christian Vocation of Forgiveness

Living a Life of Peace and Grace

DOMINICK D. HANKLE

RESOURCE *Publications* • Eugene, Oregon

THE CHRISTIAN VOCATION OF FORGIVENESS
Living a Life of Peace and Grace

Copyright © 2017 Dominick D. Hankle. All rights reserved. Except for brief quotations in critical publications or reviews, no part of this book may be reproduced in any manner without prior written permission from the publisher. Write: Permissions, Wipf and Stock Publishers, 199 W. 8th Ave., Suite 3, Eugene, OR 97401.

Resource Publications
An Imprint of Wipf and Stock Publishers
199 W. 8th Ave., Suite 3
Eugene, OR 97401

www.wipfandstock.com

PAPERBACK ISBN: 978-1-5326-0568-0
HARDCOVER ISBN: 978-1-5326-0570-3
EBOOK ISBN: 978-1-5326-0569-7

Manufactured in the U.S.A.   FEBRUARY 17, 2017

New Revised Standard Version Bible, copyright 1989, Division of Christian Education of the National Council of the Churches of Christ in the United States of America. Used by permission. All rights reserved.

This book is dedicated to my wife Andrea and my children Olivia, Hannah, and Domenic.

I am grateful for the forgiveness they have shown me in our shared life as well as teaching me what it means to truly love one another as Christ commands.

Contents

1 Why should Christians be Forgiving? | 1

    Forgiveness, Part of the Christian Vocation
    The Creation and Fall of Humanity
    Jesus Christ, the Living Forgiveness of God
    Summary of Chapter 1

2 The Characteristics of Forgiveness | 20

    Forgiveness—An Unnatural Response to Injustice
    Christ Commands Us to Forgive
    We are Forgiven as We Forgive
    Forgiveness is a Gift Received and Given
        The God Image, How Forgiveness is Shaped
            Christ—The Image of God Informing Our God Image
    Forgiveness is Not Reconciliation
    Summary of Chapter 2

3 Forgiveness in the Early Christian Community | 50

    The Early Christian Life as a New Family
    The Early Christian Community—The Body of Christ
    The Center of a Community—Christ
    Live in Love—The Bond of Community
    Summary of Chapter 3

Contents

4 A Psychological and Theological Look at Forgiveness | 71
   Can We Really Forgive Others?
   REACH Model of Forgiveness by Everett Worthington
      Level 1—Recalling the Hurt
      Level 2—Empathize with Those Who Hurt You
      Level 3—Giving an Altruistic Gift
      Level 4—Commitment to Forgive
      Level 5—Holding on to Forgiveness
   Enright's Model of Forgiveness: Four Phases Process Model
      Some Preliminary Thoughts
      Phase I: Uncovering Your Anger
      Phase II: The Deciding Phase
      Phase III: The Work Phase of Forgiveness
      Phase IV: The Discovery Phase
   Using Theological and Psychological Insight to be a Person of Forgiveness
      Preparing to Forgive
      Making it Personal
      Making the Choice
   Summary of Chapter 4

5 Exercising Forgiveness and the Fruits of a Forgiving Life | 98
   Doing the Forgiving—Allowing the Holy Spirit to Clarify your Pain
   Doing the Forgiving—Releasing the Anger
   A Concise Path to the Practice of Forgiveness
      Step 1: Committing to a Christian Worldview
      Step 2: Understanding Why You Were Hurt
      Step 3: Assessing Alternative to Forgiveness
      Step 4: Developing Empathy and Compassion
      Step 5: Extending Forgiveness
      Step 6: Creating Your Redemptive Narrative
      Step 7: Living Your Redemptive Narrative
   The Benefits of Forgiveness
   Summary of Chapter Five

Bibliography | *123*

1

Why Should Christians be Forgiving?

We receive a great many benefits from practicing virtue. Studies on gratitude, love, friendship, etc., are all areas of interest for a movement called positive psychology. This branch of psychology has built a body of evidence regarding the benefits of virtuous living. I applaud this work but caution Christians to remember there's more to the exercise of virtue than immediate psychological and emotional benefits. The practice of virtue is about more than accommodating our personal well-being, it has to do with our vocation as Christians. While Christians should be grateful the practice of virtue benefits their personal lives, we also need to be mindful of the eternal perspective virtuous living embraces. This is especially true with forgiveness. It's my hope this first chapter explains why forgiveness matters regardless of its effects on the quality of our lives in the here and now. We must understand forgiveness as something done in response to our calling. Let's explore that idea a little more in the following pages.

FORGIVENESS, PART OF THE CHRISTIAN VOCATION

To understand why forgiveness matters we need to explore the concept of vocation. In particular, we need to understand the difference between a general vocation and a specific vocation. Let me use my life as an example to help explain these two different but related concepts. I serve the Lord through a number of particular vocations. First, I work as a psychology professor at a Christian university. That's a particular vocation at a particular place in which I serve the Kingdom of God by educating students in the discipline of psychology. In addition to my job as a psychology professor I'm an ordained minister in a particular church body. That again is a particular vocation in which I serve a particular part of the body of Christ. Yet, within all these particular vocations there is a general vocation I exercise simply because I'm a Christian. Part of this general Christian vocation includes the idea I am an incarnational representation of forgiveness within the family and communities I live. To be Christian is to be a living sign of the forgiveness and reconciliation Christ offers the world.

For the Christian, a vocation is a response to a divine call. A vocation finds its source in God, not the individual. It's a God given call (Thus the English word derives its meaning from the Latin word *vocare* which means to call) to which one must respond. The individual must respond but the response must be discerned through a number of channels, one in particular is the Christian community. The community is part of the discernment process because when we talk about particular vocations it's within a communal context the individual serves. A particular vocation is always mediated through a faith community. Ministry is a perfect example because most Christians cannot simply proclaim themselves as pastors for a non-existent church. There's always a community participating in the individual's discernment regarding whether or not they are truly experiencing a call to ministry. This community might be the local church, a larger church body, or a seminary faculty. All of these are communities of people helping individuals discern whether or not what they believe their calling is comes from God or their own psychological processes.

While our particular vocations take time to process and are discerned through a number of channels, our common vocation is much more evident. By surrendering to Christ, we immediately understand we must live our lives differently than before as a response to that surrender. We may not do it perfectly, but there's an obvious change caused by the Holy Spirit convicting us of the new life we've embraced and the sense this life means living differently. This common vocation requires us to love and serve God above all else and place ourselves at the service of others. Vocation in the Christian sense has ontological implications as well as functional implications. It's a type of "being" manifested in "doing." The Christian "takes back" his or her human dignity by choosing a life of grace instead of a natural life impacted by sin. Because we're made in the image and likeness of God, a human life is best lived when it reflects the divine life in this fallen world. The Christian regains (Through grace) a special human dignity and lives in this dignified manner through acts of love toward God and neighbor. To live the general Christian vocation is to live as Christ demonstrates in Matthew 5:13–16:

> You are the salt of the earth; but if salt has lost its taste, how can its saltiness be restored? It is no longer good for anything, but is thrown out and trampled under foot. You are the light of the world. A city built on a hill cannot be hidden. No one after lighting a lamp puts it under the bushel basket, but on the lampstand, and it gives light to all in the house. In the same way, let your light shine before others, so that they may see your good works and give glory to your Father in heaven.

This passage is a reminder God intends us to live lives incarnationally reflecting the divine life as a transforming agent making this world more perfectly reflect the coming Kingdom of God. Part of the Christian's common vocation is to live kingdom values in the world. God intended human beings to live virtuously as benevolent caretakers of creation giving him glory and praise. In our fallen state we're content to live creaturely instead of grace filled divinely ordered lives. We prefer living in darkness rather than in light. The virtuous life is deemed useless because it benefits others more than us. The light of kingdom values gets covered up and never gives the world the guidance it needs, the guidance we're intended to provide as God's caretakers of creation. People choose to be something they were never intended to be with every selfish act they perform. The Christian vocation calls us to recognize we've been "Fearfully and wonderfully made" (Psalm 139:14) and we are "Little less than the angels" (Hebrews 2:7). Sin has caused us to forget our true nature and embrace our creaturely, selfish, unfruitful lives instead of the grace filled lives God intended us to live.

To explore how we've come to such a sad condition it's important to revisit the narrative of salvation outlined in the bible. Let's look at that narrative now to lay a foundation for understanding why we must be agents of forgiveness if we call ourselves Christian.

THE CREATION AND FALL OF HUMANITY

Christianity is about relationships. It's about the connections people make between God, one another, and the created order. This understanding of Christianity is most perfectly reflected in the concept of the Trinity. The Trinity is uniquely Christian. This triune concept of God makes Christianity different from other monotheistic religions. The Trinity describes the Godhead as one God consisting of three divine persons. God is one, but also three, reflecting not simply a lone God in the universe but a divine communion of love. Therefore, those created in his image are also created for relationships. The Christian faith knows God as a divine communion of three persons each distinct from the other yet consisting of the same divine substance. Everything begins and proceeds from the Father the creator of heaven and earth. Coexisting with God the Father is God the Son, the eternal Word from which the Father speaks creation into existence. This eternal Word became incarnate as Jesus Christ the one who perfectly reveals the Father's will for all humanity. God the Father intensely loves God the Son and gives all of creation to the Son as an act of selfless giving and grace. The Son eternally receives the gift of creation but in a completely selfless act lovingly returns it to the Father in adoration for all the Father is and does. This continual act of receiving and giving in pure love is a type of dance; a unified process from which flows the Holy Spirit, the loving essence of the internal life of the Trinity. God within himself is distinctly three persons, the Father who creates, the Son who adores the Father, and the Holy Spirit personifying the loving action within the Godhead. The Holy Spirit is not merely a force but a divine person proceeding from the Father. These three persons are related in such a loving union they exist as one God. The mystery of the Trinity can be described as one God eternally existing as three divine persons yet never viewed as three distinct Gods. They share the same divine substance but are uniquely their own persons. It's hard to wrap your mind around these concepts (Thus the term mystery is applied to the concept of Trinity) but it's Christianity's understanding of the Godhead. The early Christians discussed this connection and economic manifestation constantly. Here is an example from Tertullian, a western father of the church who wrote the following in the second century:

> Thus the connection of the Father in the Son, and of the Son in the Paraclete, produces three coherent Persons, who are yet distinct One from another. These Three are one essence, not one Person, as it is said, "I and my Father are One," in respect of unity of substance, not singularity of number.[1]

Understanding this relational nature of God helps us understand something about ourselves. The key question needing answered is if we're created in the image of God existing eternally as a loving communion how is it reflected in who we are? To answer that question we need to reflect on the first few chapters of Genesis.

The first chapter of Genesis describes God creating everything we know as real. God creates the heavens, the earth, and the rest of creation as a divine craftsman ordering things perfectly. The pinnacle of his creation is the human person. God intended people, created in his image, to most perfectly reflect this image as a community, not merely as isolated individuals. The second chapter of Genesis fills in the gaps the first creation account left open by showing us the importance of the communal existence

---

1. Tertullian *Ante-Nicene Fathers volume* 3 "Against Praxeas," 621

of human beings. In the second chapter of Genesis God places Adam in a Garden where he lives and cares for the created order. God created Adam to be a good steward of creation. Additionally, Adam was meant to live a life of communion with God himself. In other words, humanity was meant to participate in the life of God by reflecting his divine image upon creation caring for and nurturing what God created. Additionally, as part of creation and its keeper people have the responsibility for taking all creation has to offer and give it back to God through praise and worship in awe of his majesty and glory (sounds a little like our reflection on the internal life of the Trinity, doesn't it?) Importantly, at this point in the narrative, God asks Adam to name all the creatures he created. While doing this Adam recognizes he's alone. It's as if God wants Adam to come to the realization with every creature he names "I am incomplete." God echoes that experience when he says in Genesis chapter 2, verse 18: "It is not good that man should be alone; I will make him a helper as his partner." Ultimately, after Adam names all of creation God creates from Adam's side a partner that will complete him. The Genesis account reads as follows (Chapter 2 verses 21 through 25):

> So the Lord God caused a deep sleep to fall upon the man, and he slept; then he took one of his ribs and closed up its place with flesh. And the rib that the Lord God had taken from the man he made into a woman and brought her to the man. Then the man said, 'This at last is bone of my bones and flesh of my flesh; this one shall be called Woman, for out of Man this one was taken.' Therefore a man leaves his father and his mother and clings to his wife, and they become one flesh. And the man and his wife were both naked and were not ashamed.

There's so much to take from these passages we could get lost in the content for decades. For now let's continue focusing on the manner in which they speak about humanity's communal nature as a reflection of the divine. The account of Adam and Eve's creation demonstrates human beings are not intended to live alone. People flourish best when they share their lives with others. By the time you get to the end of the first two chapters of Genesis you discover God the creator of all things takes joy in his creation. God is not distant and uninvolved with creation rather he delights in it describing it as good. To complete the goodness of creation God makes people rule over and care for his good work. God never intends people to use creation for destructive and selfish reasons. Humanity is meant to share in God's divine life by living in communion with him and in harmony with the rest of creation. Human beings are different from the rest of the created world because they were made to reflect the divine life of God back into the created order. To do this well God created men and women to live in a loving communion in which the two become one flesh just as the three divine persons are one God.

The stage is set. If the story stopped here all would be well. However, when we look around we certainly don't find this communion of love being expressed in the way we live today. What went wrong? Continued reflection on the narrative of Genesis provides us with the answer. Chapter three starts with a story about a serpent and the woman Eve. It's in this part of the narrative we discover how easily we can abuse the great gift of free will God blessed us with from the start of our creation.

In the beginning of time God gave humanity one law. Don't eat the fruit of one particular tree. The fruit of this tree poisons the human spirit taking away its innocence. Once it's eaten the world is understood in terms of good and evil. These forces are difficult to discern from one another because by eating this fruit the human spirit becomes disordered. Evil brings confusion while good allows for order and structure. God desires human beings to exist holistically in a state of order to live in relationship with him, not confused and "disordered" blinded by evil struggling to discover what is good. The fruit of the forbidden tree distorts humanity's ability to love. Originally human beings loved properly and in an orderly fashion; God first, then each other. After being poisoned by the fruit confusion crept into the core of humanity's existence and twisted their ability to love. Let's continue reflecting on the narrative.

Eve finds herself in a conversation with the serpent who asks her about this forbidden fruit God commanded them to avoid. Eve responds in Genesis chapter 3 verses 2 and 3, "We may eat of the fruit of the trees in the garden; but God said you shall not eat of the fruit of the tree that is in the middle of the garden, nor shall you touch it, or you shall die." Evil, represented by the serpent, is a master at twisting meaning and words around developing lies that seem reasonable and truthful. That's exactly what happens in this conversation. Evil knows how to play on the human heart drawing out selfishness, the very thing that twists love around destroying its divine characteristic and making it worldly. The serpent responds to Eve saying in verses 4 and 5, "You will not die; for God knows that when you eat of it your eyes will be opened, and you will be like God, knowing good and evil."

A simple dialog starts the unraveling process of creation. Just a few innocent words passed between two creatures have tremendous ramifications for reality. No longer believing God desires what's good for them, human beings want to "be God" instead of being "like God." Disorder strikes at the heart of their self-understanding and this seemingly innocent desire to know more shifts them further from friendship with God. Eve takes the fruit and shares it with Adam. When they eat it they no longer gaze at one another with innocent love; they gaze at one another in embarrassment because "They knew that they were naked (vs. 7)." Love, which is intended to draw people toward one another, becomes distorted causing Adam and Eve to focus on their own nakedness instead of the beauty of each other's bodies; gifts from the creator for them to enjoy. The result of this shift of focus is embarrassment. Innocence is gone. In their relationship with God, human beings no longer desired to be with God but rather became fearful of his presence. The Genesis account says in chapter 3 verse 8, "And the man and his wife hid themselves from the presence of the Lord God among the trees of the Garden." God calls out to them as a father does for his lost children. God knows where they are. He isn't ignorant of their location. God played this game of hide and seek for Adam and Eve's benefit intending to teach them something about who he is and what they had become. God was showing them even in the disorder and chaos they created by misusing their free will, he still desired to be with them. In shame Adam and Eve no longer looked for God, rather they hid from him because their love became perverted and tainted with self-interest.

God gave humanity a free will and fully appreciated its power and potential pitfalls. God knew if he was to design a creature capable of love it was necessary they possessed free will. In the account of Adam and Eve's choice to be "God" instead of being "like God" the gift of love and freedom became distorted. Natural consequences flowed from this choice. Verses 14 through 22 of chapter 3 in Genesis describe how Adam and Eve's choice unraveled the delicate order God placed in creation. First, God explains because of the choices they made human beings will exist in a constant battle with evil. The women and the serpent will live in a relationship of enmity meaning people will be in a constant battle with evil forces trying to discern what is right, good, and holy among a myriad of confusing choices. Adam and Eve's desire to "be God" instead of his image bearers created a laborious existence for humanity instead of a grace filled life of love and joy. Bringing forth life requires painful childbearing experiences and frustrating desires for one another. The original equality shared between men and women becomes distorted. The woman originally created from the side of man reflecting her equality and partnership with him now struggles for that same status as man is now given the task of ruling over her. Humanity also struggles to provide food for sustenance through hard labor and difficult work. What was once a joy and pleasure for human beings becomes a toiling job burdened by thistles and briars as the earth unwillingly gives up its fruit for our sustenance. Ultimately, the core of humanity's existence is struck by the choice to disobey God. God intended people to live with a body and soul infused together for eternity. Yet when Adam and Eve chose disobedience even that very intimate part of who they are became spoiled. After toil, work, struggle with evil, and searching for God, people die. Death separates human beings from their very selves, body and soul torn apart by the choice to live outside of God's intended purposes.

The fall from grace is multifaceted and we live its consequences today. God closed off access to eternal life and made heavenly things shadows and mysteries requiring difficult discernment to rediscover in this present state. At the end of Genesis chapter 3 God drives humanity from paradise and closes its gates. If the story ended here one might think of God as a terrible unloving father. Thankfully, the story doesn't end here but only begins at this crucial point. God has a plan to bring us back into a relationship with him. This is the story of salvation framing the Christian understanding of the world. The fall has surely made a mess of things. First, it separated our access to a full living relationship with God. We are created for that relationship but because we chose to love ourselves first, that relationship is distorted and incomplete. Every culture ever encountered in the world practices a religion. This speaks volumes about the fact we all desire God but struggle to understand how to reestablish that connection. This is the first consequence of living in a fallen world. We have become severed from God.

The second consequence of the fall is the loss of perfect relationships with one another. People struggle to love each other. Power, politics, injustice, self-interest, and a multitude of factors cause us to abuse and hurt one another constantly. There's constant division between the sexes, races, ethnic groups, and national countries perpetuating the effects of fallen human nature. We seem to be perpetually trapped in a world where human beings cannot see one another as people to be loved. It's just much simpler to see people as objects to be used so we can get what we want. The division between human beings continues.

The third effect of the fall is a division between human beings and the environment. We have a relationship of extremes with the world we inhabit. We either make it an idol in which nature is understood as more important than human beings or we denigrate it to be nothing more than disposable material for satisfying our own desires. Both positions are wrong and misguided. We cannot treat dogs as if they have eternal souls spending more energy on their conservation than on the care for children struggling to find a safe and comfortable home. Yet we also cannot take these creatures of God and breed them until they're genetically destroyed simply for profit.

The fall of humanity, a Christian idea discovered in the pages of Genesis, is continually demonstrated perpetuating itself over and over again. One generation after the other finds within itself the seeds of evil and distorted love. We continue to struggle to know God, love each other, and live harmoniously with creation. However, God doesn't leave us to falter. His love continues to insert itself into human history.

In Genesis chapter 3 verse 15 God tells the serpent, "I will put enmity between you and the woman, and between your offspring and hers; he will strike your head, and you will strike his heel." Historically, the Christian church understands this passage as the promise of a coming savior. From the time of the fall God planned to reestablish a living relationship with people, he is not a God who gives up and turns away from love. Remember, Christianity is primarily about relationships. It teaches about the proper order of relationships, first with God and then with one another, and lastly with the created order. If the Christianity you practice doesn't include a transforming loving relationship with God it's not a healthy Christian experience. You cannot make the Christian experience a group of rules and regulations. However, like all relationships there are expectations both parties have of one another that make it work. Like any love relationship intimacy with God requires particular responses and commitments. Sometimes it means not doing what we think is important so we can do what God finds important. When a married couple communicates with one another they have to learn to speak their partner's love language. If we enter a relationship with God we need to speak his love language. The Christian church has been helping the lovers of God do that for thousands of years. God hasn't hidden his love language, rather it's revealed in the scriptures and most perfectly in his son Jesus Christ. To be like Christ is to love God the Father perfectly. Christianity isn't primarily about what people should or shouldn't do (although this develops as one grows in a relationship with Christ) but primarily how one loves God and those God places in their lives.

Having pondered this, we see the primary damage of the fall is the severing of relationships. The relationship one shares with God first, with each other, and with all of creation. But as Genesis 3:15 hints, there will be a time when human beings will be able to crush the evil causing this broken situation. The offspring of "woman" will make right what is wrong. This isn't a 30-day plan, nor is it even a 30-year project. It will take generations to accomplish. Even today the work started centuries ago to correct the severed relationships is a work in progress.

To understand how this plan unfolds one has to look at the compiled books of the bible Christians call the Old Testament. This section of the bible walks through the story of how a loving God calls men and women back into a loving relationship with him. It's not an easy read; one would be imprudent to think they could skim through it or take every word presented in it as literal truth. Likewise, one would be unwise to think everything declared in these texts is nothing more than metaphor. Rather one has to read these texts as part of the greater narrative unfolding over human history. The narrative is about a God who is creator of all things desiring to live in a relationship with his creation. The capstone of his creation is the human person, made in God's image and created to live in community with him and with each other. This human person has a unique dignity above the rest of creation because of the divine image carried within its very being. Because of this unique dignity, humanity's main purpose is to give worship to God as the voice of creation and reflect God's love and concern back to one another as well as the created order. Yet, the freedom this human person has been given is and was frequently abused. This abuse of freedom caused humanity to distort the relationship they share with God, one another, and creation. Because God loves us he hasn't abandoned us and continues the dialogue of redemption making all things right. This narrative of redemption begins with a small nomadic people but grows to embrace the whole human race. We know this small group of people as the Hebrews. What we discover when reading this story is God chooses this group of people to show the world his power, majesty, holiness, and goodness. He enters into relationships with them, establishes covenants and kingdoms with them, but ultimately makes himself known to the whole world through them. It's through the Jewish nation God begins reconciling himself to humanity, humanity with one another, and humanity with creation. God uses the Jewish nation to prefigure the coming kingdom and its king. God demonstrates he can and does use people as a means of reflecting who he is and what he desires for the world. Ultimately God uses the Jewish nation to bring the world a savior. God becomes incarnate taking on human flesh and dwelling as a man among people to show us how human life is meant to be lived. This is the life Jesus Christ lives pointing us back to restored relationships. Jesus Christ is the instrument of divine forgiveness and reconciliation. As those who choose to follow him we also take on that role as a continuation of his body in the world today.

JESUS CHRIST, THE LIVING FORGIVENESS OF GOD

In Genesis 3:15 we get a sense of the corrective action God takes to undo what Adam and Eve have done through the abuse of their free will. This simple verse alludes to a time when the offspring of Eve will strike the head of the serpent. The serpent is of course Satan, the great king of lies who led Adam and Eve down this destructive path described in the fall. The offspring mentioned in this verse is of course the Son of Man and the Son of God, Jesus Christ. He is both human and divine and therefore bridges the gulf between humanity and divinity created by sin. He is the solution to the three-part illness inflicted upon all of creation by our parent's first sinful act. First, he restores our relationship with God through his sacrifice on the cross. The debt sin laid upon us is paid by Jesus Christ's perfect offering of love to the Father. Sin caused evil to penetrate all of reality and Christ chose to be the target of that evil taking upon himself the effects of sinful behavior separating us from God even though he was both holy and God incarnate. Secondly, Christ restores our relationships with one another. By becoming human God didn't merely tell us how to love and forgive one another, he showed us by entering into our human condition and loving us incarnationally. When we want to know how to live properly we need to simply look at how Christ lived and we can know what is good, holy, and beautiful. Lastly, Christ's coming showed us how to live in a restored relationship with the rest of creation. The order of love demonstrated by Jesus was to love God first, one another as we want to be loved, and then to enjoy and care for creation. Jesus didn't keep from participating in celebrations, enjoying food, wine, and the fruits of the earth. He enjoyed them in their proper measure and within their proper conditions. Creation was something to be cared for, appreciated, enjoyed, and mastered, not something evil to be avoided.

This hint in Genesis 3:15 shows us Jesus makes right what sin has distorted. He will crush sin at its source, or as the words in 3:15 say, "The serpent's head." By "head" I don't simply mean the defeat of Satan; the problem is much more complex than merely defeating the fallen angel. Christ destroys evil at its source in the human heart. When people claim him as Lord and Savior Christ transforms their human hearts. It's from the human heart evil finds its way into the world and Christ redeems even that part of who we are. The writings of the Old Testament are a preparation for the coming of Jesus Christ, the one who saves and restores. There is nothing in the prophets or the law that does not speak of Christ. Jesus reminds us of this when he says in Matthew 5:17–18, "Do not think that I have come to abolish the law or the prophets; I have come not to abolish but to fulfill. For truly I tell you, until heaven and earth pass away, not one letter, not one stroke of a letter, will pass from the law until all is accomplished." He is the fulfillment of what God revealed to the Jews. He is the savior hinted at in this small verse of Genesis.

In this passage from Matthew Jesus reminds us everything God has revealed to the chosen people of Israel is found in him.

The implication of this fulfillment is the forgiveness of God repeatedly offered to the chosen people through their worship and sacrificial offerings can now be received through Jesus Christ. How is this accomplished? By giving ourselves over to him so he may live in us and we may live in him. There is a type of transformation occurring within the life of the Christian because they accept the life of Christ in exchange for their own. We participate in the divine life of God because he humbled himself to participate in ours. It's a mysterious exchange the Christian enters into through an act of faith. This idea of exchange is exemplified in the following passage from Romans 12:1–2:

> I appeal to you therefore, brothers and sisters, by the mercies of God, to present your bodies as a living sacrifice, holy and acceptable to God, which is your spiritual worship. Do not be conformed to this world, but be transformed by the renewing of your minds, so that you may discern what is the will of God—what is good and acceptable and perfect.

Along with Romans this idea of exchanging our life for Christ's can be found in 1 Corinthians 3:16 and 1 Corinthians 6:17: "Do you not know that you are God's temple and that God's Spirit dwells in you?" (3:16), "But anyone united to the Lord becomes one spirit with him." (6:17). And again, in Galatians 2:20 we read, "and it is no longer I who live, but it is Christ who lives in me. And the life I now live in the flesh I live by faith in the Son of God, who loved me and gave himself for me." To further demonstrate this biblical idea, we can look at Philippians 1:21 "For to me, living is Christ and dying is gain." And another verse from 1 Corinthians 12:27 makes this point very clear, "Now you are the body of Christ and individually members of it." The bible is full of references demonstrating we no longer live our own life but rather we become living icons of Christ in the world. Becoming living icons of Christ is another way we reflect the God-image within ourselves. The Genesis narrative reveals the human vocation is one designed to reflect God's image to the world through its care and love while also offering sacrifice and worship to God on its behalf. Christ shows us how to do that perfectly.

When we accept the Christian way of life we are no longer simply citizens of this world but rather we become citizens of God's Kingdom. This idea is reflected in the Romans 12 passage above with its reference to not being conformed to this world. Other biblical passages like John 17:15–16 also reflect this idea. In that passage, Jesus prays, "I am not asking you to take them out of the world, but I ask you to protect them from the evil one. They do not belong to the world, just as I do not belong to the world." This implies the true home for the follower of Jesus is not in this world but in another; one in which Christ is ruler and King. We are exiles in this life making our way home in the next. This is a common metaphor for Christian living in a world still trapped in evil and sin. Remembering our dual citizenship is important given this book's topic because it helps us understand we must live as people in a Godly kingdom while dwelling as people in an earthly one. St. Augustine discusses this in Book I chapter 29 of *The City of God*:

> The whole family of God, most high and most true, has therefore a consolation of its own, a consolation which cannot deceive, and which has in it a surer hope than the tottering and falling affairs of earth can afford. They will not refuse the discipline of this temporal life, in which they are schooled for life eternal; nor will they lament their experience of it, for the good things of earth they use as pilgrims who are not detained by them, and its ills either prove or improve them.

Augustine reminds us we're pilgrims and must endure the good and bad of this life as preparation for the next. We're sojourner exiled from paradise until the work of Christ is complete. We endure the struggles of a fallen world and temperately enjoy the pleasures of this life as a foretaste of heaven. More importantly living in exile doesn't mean we escape the present world but rather we become living signs of God so the present world can be transformed into the Kingdom of God. We're active agents of love and order in the midst of hatred and chaos.

The Christian experience of exile is not unique; it's prefigured in the Jewish Babylonian exile. God asked the Jews to respond in a particular way to their exile and it's in this Jewish response Christians learn how to respond to their own exile. Remember the Jews experienced a tremendous loss of everything after their defeat by the Babylonians. Their kingdom was destroyed and they were carted off to live in a foreign land. God, speaking through the prophet Jeremiah gave them these words as a reminder of their vocation to reflect his presence in the world regardless of where they lived (Jeremiah 29:4–7):

> Thus says the Lord of hosts, the God of Israel to all the exiles whom I have sent into exile from Jerusalem to Babylon: Build houses and live in them; plant gardens and eat what they produce. Take wives and have sons and daughters; take wives for your sons, and give your daughters in marriage, that they may bear sons and daughters; multiply there, and do not decrease. But seek the welfare of the city where I have set you into exile, and pray to the Lord on its behalf, for in its welfare you will find our welfare.

This is a powerful mandate teaching a powerful lesson. The chosen people of God are meant to be living icons of his presence in a fallen world. God gave the Jews a law making them a holy people set apart for God's purposes allowing him to dwell among them. Through the prophet Jeremiah God tells the exiles he wants them to be set apart but exist within a foreign city as leaven and light making it a better place for everyone. God tells them, "I want you to live there, flourish there, and prosper but not simply for your own benefit, for the benefit of the city as well. By being active agents of prosperity and goodness you too will flourish." Basically, God is saying by being the presence of the living God these exiles will cause this foreign city to be a special place. When the city flourishes, they will be blessed and everyone will know the God of the Jews is a powerful God.

The Christian life is no different. We live in exile in a world that's not home but rather a place where we must thrive. We're not of the world but most definitely are in it for a particular reason. By living as Christ commands, we reflect the goodness of God making the world more reflective of Christ's kingdom. When we love, forgive, serve, and demonstrate virtuous lives other people are drawn to the source of this virtuous life. They want the healing peace, the shalom of God that comes from being Christian. Our vocation is to seek the welfare of this world not for selfish gain, but for the Glory of God. When we seek the welfare of this world God blesses us and the Kingdom of God is made present in a mysterious but wondrous way.

In closing this section I hope you understand the importance of Jesus Christ and the Christian life that flows from being one of his followers. While he is our individual savior he's also the example par excellance on how to live. By accepting Jesus Christ as our savior, we take on the vocation to be his presence in a broken world. It means we surrender our lives to live his life among our fellow human beings. In the next section I will articulate how we can become the living icon of God's forgiveness, one important aspect of the general Christian vocation.

SUMMARY OF CHAPTER 1

So up to this point I've tried to make a case for why being a forgiving person matters. First and foremost, it matters because as a Christian you've taken upon yourself the vocation to be an incarnational sign of the forgiving and reconciling work of God in a fallen and broken world. Where Christianity exists, forgiveness, reconciliation, and transformation should be evident. If it's not, we're not living Christian lives. The church cannot be an impotent institution simply taking up real estate on a city block. The church is each and every one of us living lives reflecting the inner nature of God as revealed in Jesus Christ and part of that reflection is being forgiving and loving people in a world full of hurt.

There are other reasons why forgiveness matters. We're going to see in the last section of this book what the benefits of exercising forgiveness are for us individually and collectively as a community.

You'll find it helps you heal, is beneficial for your physical and emotional lives as well as your spiritual life. It brings about the opportunity for reconciliation and the chance relationships can start the healing process. Ultimately, we will explore how simply living forgiving lives becomes an entry way for the grace of God transforming the very world in which we live.

2

The Characteristics of Forgiveness

IN THE LAST CHAPTER I provided you with a vision emphasizing forgiveness as part of our general Christian vocation. Just as Christ is the incarnational forgiving agent of God, we continue to be the incarnational body of Christ reflecting that same forgiving element of his ministry. If we call ourselves Christian we become agents of forgiveness and whenever possible conduits for reconciliation. In this chapter I describe the characteristics of forgiveness and a forgiving person. Just because we claim Christ as our Lord and Savior doesn't mean we automatically exhibit the fruits and gifts that come with our new identity. We have to tear down our old life and allow God to build a new one. Being transformed into a mature Christian parallels the journey the Israelites made after being freed from Egypt and traveling in the desert for 40 years. It took time for them to eliminate the many idols of Egypt ingrained in their lives. In fact, even after being saved from the Egyptians they longed for aspects of their life as slaves. In Exodus chapter 16 we hear them lament their former life because of hunger:

> The whole congregation of the Israelites set out from Elim; and Israel came to the wilderness of Sin, which is between Elim and Sinai, on the fifteenth day of the second month after they had departed from the land of Egypt. The whole congregation of the Israelites complained against Moses and Aaron in the wilderness. The

> Israelites said to them, "If only we had died by the hand of the LORD in the land of Egypt, when we sat by the fleshpots and ate our fill of bread; for you have brought us out into this wilderness to kill this whole assembly with hunger."

Being saved from a life of slavery didn't mean the life of slavery was far from their hearts. Christians have a similar struggle. Being saved from a life of slavery to sin doesn't mean the life of sin is no longer in us. This old life must die so we can embrace the new one. To develop a life of forgiveness requires letting the life of bitterness and revenge die to our new life in Christ.

I will provide some practical steps for growing a forgiving heart based on scripture and a number of psychological studies as we progress through the book. Let's start by looking over what forgiveness looks like from a biblical perspective. Because there are so many misconceptions about forgiveness it's important we clarify exactly what we mean when talking about it.

FORGIVENESS—AN UNNATURAL RESPONSE TO INJUSTICE

First, we have to understand forgiveness is not something we naturally embrace. It takes work to be forgiving because our natural response to being hurt is to strike back. It takes God's grace to be a forgiving person. This happens for a number of reasons, but the root of this reaction is our desire for justice. When we or someone we care about has been treated unjustly it stirs up strong emotions demanding satisfaction. While being angry about unjust behavior is acceptable, how we respond has to be tempered with grace. In fact, feeling angry toward unjust acts demonstrates our connection to God's revelation of justice. Jesus himself became angry at unjust acts. In Mark 11:15 Jesus is angry at the systematized style of worship emerging in the temple during his life. He knew those profiting from the system were acting unjustly toward God and other Jewish worshipers. Jesus turned over the tables of the money changers and rebuked them for their unjust behaviors:

> Then they came to Jerusalem. And he entered the temple and began to drive out those who were selling and those who were buying in the temple, and he overturned the tables of the money changers and the seats of those who sold doves; and he would not allow anyone to carry anything through the temple. He was teaching and saying, "Is it not written, My house shall be called a house of prayer for all the nations'? But you have made it a den of robbers."

Jesus shows anger at the Jews who kept the law rather than living the law. The law demands helping those in need and being a blessing to the poor and the struggling. It was never meant to be a hindrance to love. The Jewish leaders ignored the heart of the law using it to support their unjust behaviors. We read in Mark 3:4–6 the following example:

> Then he said to them, "Is it lawful to do good or to do harm on the sabbath, to save life or to kill?" But they were silent. He looked around at them with anger; he was grieved at their hardness of heart and said to the man, "Stretch out your hand." He stretched it out, and his hand was restored. The Pharisees went out and immediately conspired with the Herodians against him, how to destroy him.

When someone hurts us or those we care about we get angry. Too often people think being a forgiving person means giving up anger. Anger, when directed at unjust acts is one way we reflect the image of God. He places in our hearts a rudimentary understanding and desire for justice. As our faith matures we come to understand the nature of justice and as we experience its absence it bothers us. The desire for justice is part of the Christian experience of knowing a just God. We seek justice because being just reflects the Holy Spirit working in us. The scriptures speak to God's desire for us to be people of justice. In Isaiah 1:17 the prophet says, "Learn to do good; seek justice, rescue the oppressed, defend the orphan, plead for the widow." Once cannot forget the most frequently quoted line from the prophet Micah (Micah 3:8) where we are reminded of the importance to seek justice, "He has told you, O mortal, what is good; and what does the LORD require of you but to do justice, and to love kindness, and to walk humbly with your God?" And finally, in Psalm 106 verse three we read "Happy are those who observe justice, who do righteousness at all times." This theme of seeking justice permeates the scriptures. Our desire for justice and our anger toward what is unjust is part of who we are. Yet, we must be careful when seeking justice. Like all the sentiments and feelings in our heart, our sense of justice is distorted. Just as sin distorts our understanding of love it also distorts our understanding of justice. That's why we need forgiveness. Forgiveness gives our imperfect sense of justice a chance to be tempered through a grace filled act initiated by God. We must allow God to administer justice while we embrace forgiveness. Because we are finite creatures we can only understand justice from a finite perspective. Only God understands perfect justice and perfect mercy. God is all powerful, all knowing, and all loving. Being insufficiently resourceful, limited in knowledge, and conditionally loving is not in the nature of God as it is in us. We are limited in all these ways and therefore cannot perfectly execute justice or show perfect mercy. Only God can be truly merciful and just at the same time. We often seek revenge masked as justice. This is why scripture teaches us: "Beloved, never avenge yourselves, but leave room for the wrath of God; for it is written, "Vengeance is mine, I will repay, says the Lord." (Romans 12:9). If we need to avoid vengeance and find other ways to cope with feelings of anger, what can we do? We can forgive! Anger is an emotion and when we're treated unjustly it rises up in us as the sun in the eastern sky. Acting on these feelings can be a mistake because we don't fully understand why someone did what they did nor can we perfectly love the one who committed the action that hurt us. Perfect love and knowledge is required to learn the motives and reasons behind someone's hurtful acts. Perfect love motivates us to care enough to understand the pain and sin people carry around in their hearts causing them to act in unjust ways. Perfect love and knowledge is able to explore the imperfect causes behind someone's hurtful actions and inflames the desire to help them heal from whatever is affecting them. Only God can act in such a perfect way. But God asks us to respond in a forgiving way. This may not be our immediate response, but if we can extend forgiveness we can begin to reverse the evil consuming the world with each unjust act inflicted upon one another.

CHRIST COMMANDS US TO FORGIVE

Forgiveness, like love is a choice. As noted above it's not something that comes naturally to us rather something we must learn. Just as we love because God loved us first (1 John 4:19) we forgive because God forgives us first. Because God has blessed us with a free will that free will must be exercised in a manner giving glory to him. We do that by choosing the things that reflect who he is in our lives. In a sense, forgiving is a free will choice intimately connected to love.

I used to enjoy arguing with people who didn't believe in the gospel as fervently as I did. I was less an evangelist and more of a "gospel terrorist." My life changed drastically when the very church I was defending turned on me and treated me very callously in a time of need and vulnerability. It made me think really hard about how to treat other people, particularly those who didn't believe as I believed. It made me realize I needed to start by loving them first. I made a decision no matter how different they were from me or didn't believe as I did, I would love them first and then allow God to use me as he desired. Forgiveness is a similar process. Forgiveness requires us to make a choice to extend love and good will toward another person. It requires finding a way to love the person first and then to let God do what he will in their lives.

When we forgive, we extend as much love and goodwill as possible toward the one who hurt us. In this way, we're exercising our vocation as images of God's love in a world of hurt and destruction. Forgiveness is an act of obedience. It's a choice to do something our natural self believes foolish. Forgiveness is intimately connected to the commandment to love our neighbor, even when that neighbor is acting unjustly and hurtfully. That's why forgiveness comes from a heart of obedience. Our natural tendency is to hurt the one who hurt us however when we are obedient to God we choose to extend charity toward that individual. In Colossians 3:13 Paul clearly asks his community to be forgiving in obedience to God. He writes: "Bear with one another and, if anyone has a complaint against another, forgive each other; just as the Lord has forgiven you, so you also must forgive." And to remind us that forgiveness is a process of growing in grace and not a natural choice, Paul writes the following to the Philippians (1:6): "I am confident of this, that the one who began a good work among you will bring it to completion by the day of Jesus Christ." God asks us to be obedient and just as we're commanded to love we're commanded to extend love and goodwill to those who hurt us. Christ reminded us in Matthew 5:47 that to love only those who love us is nothing special, even the gentiles do that. To love those who are unlovable is the Christian vocation. This extending of good will and love is the heart of forgiveness.

WE ARE FORGIVEN AS WE FORGIVE

The spiritual life is one of paradox. We see the use of paradox in the bible in verses like Matthew 10:39: "Those who find their life will lose it, and those who lose their life for my sake will find it." The bible is full of these expressions. By using paradox what's said in the bible transcends our intellect and sinks into our souls. We understand the deeper truths they convey because paradox disarms our critical thinking processes forcing us to think in a fresh new way. Phrases like the one above in Matthew force us to ask questions like, "In what way do I need to lose my life for the sake of Jesus?" Spiritual paradoxes are powerful ways to get people to think more richly about God's truth.

Studying forgiveness leads us into a world of spiritual paradoxes. The scriptures are full of references to the reciprocal nature inherent in the forgiving life. Let me provide you with examples so we can look more closely at this interesting spiritual revelation: "For if you forgive others their trespasses, your heavenly Father will also forgive you; but if you do not forgive others, neither will your Father forgive your trespasses." (Matthew 6:14–15) Another passage says: "Whenever you stand praying, forgive, if you have anything against anyone; so that your Father in heaven may also forgive you your trespasses." (Mark 11:25) These passages imply God will forgive us only to the degree we forgive others. If you're like me, the idea God only forgives me as I forgive others is uncomfortable and makes me think a great deal about the nature of God. In the Lord's Prayer, we say, "Forgive us our trespasses as we forgive those who trespass against us" causing us to wonder, "Is that all God will do; forgive me as I forgive others?" Because forgiveness is not something that comes easily to me I begin to wonder about the forgiveness I have from God! Is God only as forgiving as I am? I'm a broken struggling human being and God only forgives me in the manner this broken soul can forgive others? On the surface that sounds very troubling.

To wrap our minds around this we need to think about the nature of God. Most theologians argue God is all knowing, all loving, and all-powerful. We saw that when we described why only God could be perfectly just and merciful at the same time. If we're saying this all loving God only forgives us in the same way limited forgiving people can than there's an inconsistency in our understanding of the nature of God. Yet scripture is teaching us something about the reciprocal nature of forgiveness we can't ignore.

Mother Teresa of Calcutta addressed the 1982 graduates at Thomas Aquinas University with the following words:

> And this, the joy of the presence of Jesus, you must be able to give wherever you go. But you cannot give what you don't have. That's why you need a pure heart, a pure heart that you will receive as a fruit of your prayer, as a fruit of your oneness with Christ. And a pure heart can see God. And if you see God immediately, immediately you begin to love one another. That's all Jesus came on this earth to give us, that good news: "Love as I have loved you; love one another as I have loved you."[1]

1. "St. Teresa of Calcutta's Commencement Address to the Class of 1982"

In this spiritually packed address Mother Teresa unfolds a beautiful mystery about the spiritual life we need to ponder given our present topic. Just as an all-loving God extends an overabundance of love for us to experience he also extends an overabundance of forgiveness. However, just as being loved means accepting that love from God so does being forgiven require us to accept that forgiveness from God. How do we accept the forgiveness and love of God? We accept Jesus the incarnational expression of God's love and forgiveness. By accepting Jesus as the incarnational expression of God we accept love and forgiveness from the Father. Then, as we receive this love and forgiveness we extend it to others. Mother Teresa states it very plainly, "You cannot give what you don't have." When God says he only forgives us as much as we forgive others he's reminding us any limitations we experience in forgiving exists because we haven't accepted the abundance of forgiveness he offers. To be a forgiving soul I need to understand how completely God has forgiven me. This is why it's important to reflect on our failures. We don't reflect on failures to become spiritual masochists, rather we do so to understand the great love and mercy God extends to us by meeting us in our broken fallen state. When we see how far we are from God we appreciate how far he stretches himself to be with us. We are deeply loved and deeply forgiven. Receiving that gift allows us to forgive ourselves. We must forgive ourselves as a result of the great love and forgiveness God pours into us so we can love and forgive others.

God is not limiting his forgiveness because we limit ours. God is teaching us the manner in which we forgive others is a direct reflection of the manner in which we receive his forgiveness. When we ask God to "Forgive us our trespasses as we forgive others" we're not asking for our reward. We're asking God to help us understand the more forgiving we are toward others is a direct reflection of our acceptance of his forgiveness. You cannot give what you do not have; these are powerful words in relation to love and forgiveness. When we have Jesus Christ in our lives and really understand the depth and breadth of that relationship, we can forgive and love abundantly. Reflecting on our struggle with forgiveness and love helps us recognize the difficulty we have in receiving love and forgiveness from God. For now my intention is to have you at least recognize how this paradox is part of the characteristics of forgiveness.

FORGIVENESS IS A GIFT RECEIVED AND GIVEN

We've seen God forgives us unconditionally as a pure act of love. God's love and forgiveness are gifts we freely receive, nothing we need to earn. Just as salvation is a pure act of grace, God's forgiveness is a gracious act from a loving creator. What are we expected to do with this gracious gift? Give it away. We're meant to share God's blessings with others not hoard them and keep them to ourselves. We can't be afraid of running out of love, forgiveness, grace, etc. Unlike material blessings spiritual blessings are so abundant they can never be exhausted. Yet we hang on to them like Scrooge hangs on to every coin he receives in Charles Dickens tale "*A Christmas Carol.*" One thing I want you to take away from this section of the book is the importance of learning to give away the love and forgiveness God gives you. Being comfortable giving love and forgiveness away requires acknowledging the abundance of these gifts in your own life. We know God's love and forgiveness are abundant because we know God's love and forgiveness flow from an endless ocean of grace.

How we understand the character of God impacts how generous we are with his gifts. If we think of God as nothing more than a grandfather rewarding his good grandchildren with love and his bad grandchildren with punishment, we're going to struggle to give away the love and forgiveness we receive from him. We're going to think giving away his love means having to earn it back again later. This is an unhealthy God image some of us carry around in our minds and impacts our ability to love others and forgive them when they hurt us. Because our God image is so powerful we need to have a discussion about this topic. Let's explore how our image of God reflects our ability to forgive. Remember the previous discussion about giving away what we do not have? The more we recognize the love and forgiveness God has for us the more we can be forgiving and loving toward others. Appreciating the abundant forgiveness and love God has for us allows us to be forgiving and loving toward others. The image you have of God dictates your understanding of how much he loves and forgives you.

The God Image, How Forgiveness is Shaped

A God image is something each of us carries around in our mind. It's a psychological construct packed with emotional components and profoundly impacts our spiritual and psychological lives. For our purposes, we're going to explore how our God image impacts our ability to be a forgiving person. By no means am I saying a God image means there is no God. I'm also not saying we have no way of knowing the true nature of God and therefore construct a God image to take God's place. What I'm trying to make clear is because of sin we construct a psychological representation of God which is usually incorrect and keeps us from experiencing God as he truly is. When sin impacts our understanding of God's loving and forgiving nature it distorts our ability to draw on him as a source of grace, love, and forgiveness.

According to most psychoanalytical traditions, we develop our God image from a variety of sources. These sources include experiences with various authority figures over our lifetime. It may involve experiences with family, friends, parents, and official religious representatives. The God image is shaped by religious traditions, practices, and culture. Additionally, the God image may include projected material; the things about ourselves we have difficulty accepting and more easily attribute to God. These attributes don't have to be negative in nature, just something we have difficulty attributing to ourselves. For example, a man who is tender hearted may not often show that side of himself because when he does he believes he's weak. He wants to be known as tough, rugged, and stone hearted so any behavior contradicting that image can't be a part of his nature but rather God working in him. All of these sources are said to converge upon the individual's psychological world and form a God Image.

It should be noted the God image is different from the God concept. The God concept is the intellectual understanding of God and his characteristics. To describe things more simply, we might say we can have an idea of who God is in our minds but it may not fit well with our God image, the psychological representation of God directing our unconscious inferences and tensions. While our intellectual understanding of God can be consciously recalled to formulate apologetical arguments, our God image has the potential to subconsciously direct how we engage our inner and outer world. Our God image may infer a positive, supportive, and perhaps challenging God or it may offer our psyche a God who is punitive, distant, and uninvolved. This distinction is important to remember as we explore our topic of forgiveness. While we may understand the characteristics of God as they relate to forgiving others, how we engage God, his grace, etc., these may not be congruent with how we experience God. Remember the reciprocal relationship of feeling forgiven and forgiving others can really impact how we live a life of forgiveness. If I cannot accept that God forgives me even though I can intellectually understand he is all forgiving my God image impacts my ability to exercise forgiveness. The God image is more of an emotional experience of God than it is an intellectual understanding of God.

A God image can be quite diverse. Many psychoanalytic researchers believe it can become compensatory in nature or correspond with parental characteristics. For example, as an individual develops the God image may provide a parental presence when one was absent. Additionally, the God image can correspond with a proactive nurturing parental image in a family structure where parents provided appropriate care and attention. Yet, the God image may also correspond with negative experiences creating in the individual a concept of God as punitive, uncaring, and angry. Ultimately the God image tends to fall into three categories. The first is one in which God is active, benevolent, guiding, stable, omniscient, and omnipresent. A second views God as severe, wrathful, and condemning. Lastly, God is thought to be distant, uncaring, deistic-like, impersonal, passive, irrelevant, etc. This last category regards God as a supernatural force. While these are general categories it's not uncommon to have some crossover between them creating multiple configurations of a God image. These different God images can impact a number of behaviors and attitudes expressed in our lives. If God is good, benevolent, and a guiding force one tends to exhibit pro-social and positive relational characteristics when interacting with others. If he is distant, irrelevant, and impersonal, God is viewed as a force to be manipulated or ignored and therefore interactions with others become utilitarian and unimportant. Of course, these are general observations, but nonetheless the idea remains if we carry around a particular God image there are ramifications in the manner we engage the world around us.

Why is this important for our discussion about the gift of forgiveness? If we're carrying around a poorly formed God image, we may not exercise forgiveness in a biblical or psychologically healthy way because we have a skewed understanding of the gift giver. If I experience God as uninvolved in the created order and simply that magical clock maker setting things into motion, how can I believe he is personally involved in forgiving me? From there I might ask why then, should I care if I forgive others? If God is involved in this world but wrathful and condemning, then I better cower under his punishment and work really hard to follow his law. It's not up to me to forgive others, only God does that and if he is a God of wrath, they better make good on what they've done. If I'm made in the image of a wrathful God then the forgiveness I extend must reflect the forgiveness of the wrathful king I know him to be. I must be just, swift in execution of punishment, and only forgiving once justice has been satisfied. If you follow my example you find there is no unconditional love in this wrathful God image, only juridical satisfaction. So yes, God image is important for us to understand because it impacts how we execute and extend this gift of forgiveness.

So, what is a healthy God image? I think we've touched on that already, but let's sum things up again so we can explore a biblically correct God image reflecting who God really is. Many people like to turn to the Old Testament to justify a wrathful and punitive God image. They argue we cannot ignore biblical verses like these: "I will execute great vengeance on them with wrathful punishments. Then they shall know that I am the Lord, when I lay my vengeance on them." (Ezekiel 25:17) Another passage echoing the same theme regarding the wrathful nature of God is found in Nahum 1:2–6:

> A jealous and avenging God is the Lord, the Lord is avenging and wrathful; the Lord takes vengeance on his adversaries and rages against his enemies. The Lord is slow to anger but great in power, and the Lord will by no means clear the guilty. His way is in whirlwind and storm, and the clouds are the dust of his feet. He rebukes the sea and makes it dry, and he dries up all the rivers; Bashan and Carmel wither, and the bloom of Lebanon fades. The mountains quake before him, and the hills melt; the earth heaves before him, the world and all who live in it. Who can stand before his indignation? Who can endure the heat of his anger. His wrath is poured out like fire, and by him the rocks are broken in pieces.

The bible is full of images like these. Does that mean we settle on this characteristic as representative of God? Do we form a God image only on the idea that he is wrathful and punitive? If you combine that with life experiences in a home where parents are distant and punitive, or in work conditions where authority figures lord their power over you insisting on rules regardless of the context of a situation you may create a punitive wrathful God image that reflects these scripture passages.

Scripture paints another picture of God as well. In other parts of the bible we find a loving God who treats those he loves tenderly. Again, here are a couple of passages from scripture giving us another picture of God. The first is found in Isaiah 63:7, "I will recount the gracious deeds of the Lord, the praiseworthy acts of the Lord, because of all that the Lord has done for us, and the great favor to the house of Israel that he has shown them according to his mercy, according to the abundance of his steadfast love." To further illustrate this loving merciful image from the Old Testament, look at Nehemiah 9:17, "they refused to obey, and were not mindful of the wonders that you performed among them; but they stiffened their necks and determined to return to their slavery in Egypt. But you are a God ready to forgive, gracious and merciful, slow to anger and abounding in steadfast love, and you did not forsake them." In these passages, we encounter a God of love and mercy. This image of God leads us to be people who forgive unconditionally extending love in the same way God extends it to us. While this approach sounds good, it can also be taken too far making us seem like people high on some drug responding to unjust acts as if we're numb to the pain they cause. Someone only focusing on the loving image of God might walk around saying "It's okay, I understand and forgive you. God is love and that's all that matters." Love, love, love, mercy, mercy, mercy, that's all God is. We run into a multitude of problems if this is the only God image we have because then there's no sin; nothing damaging our relationship with God and one another. No matter how much we sin, God is there to forgive us whether we ask for his forgiveness or not. No matter how little we repent or are convicted of our sin, God is there to forgive us. This God image can be as damaging as one where God is completely punitive in nature.

Given all we have said thus far, how can we really understand what God is like? I specifically chose passages from the Old Testament to describe God because while these passages speak the truth about God's characteristics, they are incomplete. Christianity proposes if one is to fully know God they must come into a relationship with Jesus Christ. When we know Jesus Christ the Holy Spirit convicts us of the true nature of God. To know the Father, we must know the Son. By knowing the Son, we have access to the Father. If our God image is skewed, it's because it's incongruent with knowledge of Jesus Christ the full revelation of God. Jesus reminds us no one knows the Father except the Son and those the son chooses

(Matthew 11:27). When asked to show the disciples the Father Christ reminded them to know him is to know the Father (John 14:7–8). So, if we really want to know the characteristics of God we need to know Christ. A perfected God image is developed by focusing on Christ. Let's briefly examine the scriptures to identify who Christ is particularly in the context of our topic, forgiveness. In this way, we can have a clear biblical understanding of the giver of this gift of forgiveness.

Christ—The Image of God Informing Our God Image

To really know what God is like Christians believe you have to know what Jesus is like. The Christian tradition believes Christ is the incarnational presence of God Himself. In order to develop a congruent God image, we need solid information that can override the skewed God image we develop because of environmental factors such as poor parenting, indifferent authority figures, or too much exposure to sin and evil numbing us to the continuous love and care God offers. In order to develop that congruent accurate God image, we need to ask ourselves what the scriptures say about the character of Christ. When I have a better understanding of who Christ is I have a more accurate understanding of who God is. I need to know Christ to make sense of the wrathful God described in one place and the loving God described in another. Both of these experiences exist in the Jewish mind, but how has Christ caused these images to converge and present themselves in the New Testament? How does Jesus, the fulfillment of the prophets and the law give me a more complete picture of God? The best way to approach this is by exploring the scriptures to develop a well-rounded understanding of the characteristics of Christ. From there we may develop a better understanding of God the Father. While not comprehensive, the scriptural sources I use below give us some understanding of who Christ is so this knowledge can inform our God image.

I believe there are eight specific characteristics of Christ that allow the diverse images of God in the old testament to converge into a clearer understanding of who God is as revealed in Christ. These eight characteristics are building blocks for a Christian's understanding of his or her God image. These characteristics of Christ are, he is loving, patient, faithful, Just, generous, holy, forgiving, and compassionate. Let's look at each of these in some detail to explore how they inform our God image.

There are two scripture verses that speak profoundly to the fact Christ is loving but like a number of these characteristics we can find them permeating all of scripture. The first can be found in the Gospel of John, which teaches God's very nature is love. In John 13:1 we read the following: "Now before the festival of the Passover, Jesus knew that his hour had come to depart from this world and go to the Father. Having loved his own who were in the world, he loved them to the end." My favorite line in this passage is, "He loved them to the end." John reminds us the primary motivating force for Jesus Christ is his love for the very people he created. Unlike Jesus, we love people conditionally. We're capable of unconditional love, but sin keeps us from expressing love so graciously and unconditionally that we seldom know it when we see it. We tend to love in an almost utilitarian fashion. An individual may treat you a particular way or function in your life in a certain capacity so you love them. I make you feel a certain way and therefore as long as I do that you love me. Yet with Christ, no matter what we do, how we behave, or the manner in which we love Christ back, he loves us to the end. Until we take our last breath Christ is extending his love toward us. All we need to do is accept it.

Christ's love is sacrificial in nature, never selfish and comes at a great personal cost. Paul reminds us of this selfless sacrificial love when he writes in Galatians 2:20: " and it is no longer I who live, but it is Christ who lives in me. And the life I now live in the flesh I live by faith in the Son of God, who loved me and gave himself for me." Think about this; the very God who is master and creator of the universe offers himself completely for you because he can do nothing else but love. Love requires all of whom one is to be perfect love and that's the kind of love Jesus offers. It's safe to say these two passages echo the core characteristic of God as being loving. Jesus Christ shows us his love in his sacrificial offering of himself. God the Father can be understood as a selfless loving God as exemplified in the person of Jesus Christ. Perhaps it's human weakness keeping us from experiencing this kind of love. We've been so hurt, tormented by the hate and evil of others, and scarred by the pain these experiences left on us we cannot believe there is a God who can love us in our miserable condition. Yet there is such a love offered and that love is Jesus Christ.

Patience is another characteristic of God evident in the person of Christ. Our God does not act impulsively rather he is exceptionally tolerant of our ignorance and hard heartedness. The patience of Christ is easily found in Luke chapter 9:41: "Jesus answered, "You faithless and perverse generation, how much longer must I be with you and bear with you?"

Passages like this really bring home the fact Christ was not just divine, but human as well. Let's think about the context in which the above words were said. Peter and the other disciples have come to an understanding that Jesus is the Messiah, the Son of God transfigured in front of them revealing his divinity. His glory shined through his human form and God spoke to them saying Jesus was his only and beloved Son. In this marvelous event heaven broke forth into the temporal world and God spoke. We can only imagine how powerful an experience this was for the disciples. Then, as they came off the mountain they were quickly reminded of the darkness and confusion surrounding them. A man brings his son to the disciples who remained behind waiting for Christ and the others to return. When Christ arrives, he discovers confusion and chaos among them. The disciples claimed evil is too great for them to conquer because they could not help the man and his son. The man was losing hope that this Christian message proclaimed by these disciples had any power to cure his son at all. None of these followers of Jesus seemed to be able to help his child. Crowds fixated on the miracles and signs without recognizing the Kingdom of God is so much more than a magic show. Yet Christ saw an immediate need to help a young man struggling with spiritual possession and cured him even though his miracles were about more than just helping people with their immediate problems.

As a college professor, I can certainly understand the frustration welling up inside Jesus. All his teaching, the example of his life and ministry, everything he did to help form them into disciples seems to have been for nothing! When I spend a great deal of time presenting concepts, ideas, and giving examples I expect students to catch on at some point. When they don't, I want to scream saying, "Okay, it's obvious your high school experience never trained you to think so I'm going to start again with the basics. I had no intention of teaching these simple elements about the topic and assumed you already knew them! Let's try this again dummies!" That's not what Christ does (Nor do I by the grace of God). Certainly, in his human nature he experiences some discouragement regarding how little his disciples have retained, but he continues forming them into the people he needs to carry out the Gospel mission. In fact, after he heals the young man the rest of chapter nine describes how he taught them more of the basic concepts about who he is and what his mission involves. He discusses his coming death, provides more information about true servant leadership, speaks about receiving others who do good things in his name, how to handle those rejecting his message, and what a true follower of the Gospel lives like. None of these are new teachings, and if you look at the Gospel up to this point Christ has touched on these themes before. Yet, because he knows his disciples still don't get it, he patiently teaches them again, and again, and again. By being patient he teaches us the need for patience in dealing with one another.

Luke is not the only one to record Christ's patient disposition. Matthew records Jesus' comment to the disciples still struggling to understand his parables in chapter 15 verse 16: "Then he said, "Are you also still without understanding?" Jesus has just explained the importance of ignoring the Pharisees teaching because they focus on the letter of the law without understanding its depth and purpose. Peter thinks Jesus was a little insulting and reminds him his words were offensive to the Pharisees. Jesus tells Peter to pay attention to what comes out of our mouths because it's in the words we speak that we make things unclean, not through the things we eat. Peter just doesn't get it. Instead of throwing his hands up and saying, "You guys are just too stupid to follow me, I need to find another group with higher IQs", Jesus steps back, patiently looks at them and says, "Okay, here is what the parable means." Jesus' divine nature of pure grace remains even when we frustrate his human nature. His patience is not just in his teaching but as we can imagine is in his forgiveness as well. This patient forgiveness reflects the heart of God the Father.

The third characteristic to explore is the faithfulness of Jesus. God's faithfulness is truly revealed in the person of Jesus Christ. He doesn't desert us or leave us; rather he is ever faithfully present. The problem in the "God-us" relationship is not that God deserts us, rather we desert him. We're often confused because in our limited human experience we think when things don't go our way God has left us. Many Old Testament authors articulate this human experience when they speak of God turning his back on them (Psalm 22), being asleep when they need him (Psalm 44:23), or not being mindful of the promises he made with them (Psalm 42:9). These laments are human cries to a God we can't fully understand and must trust in faith. Paul also uses this type of language in Romans when in chapter one he declares, "God gave them up" as the result of a number of sins humanity committed. Paul, like the authors of the Old Testament, is merely speaking from a human understanding attempting to describe the experience of a God who seems distant and unavailable to the unrepentant sinner. This experience is real and recorded throughout the bible, which leaves us asking, is God really as faithful as we think?

We need to return to Jesus' comments to obtain a clear understanding of the faithfulness of God. There is no contradiction in the scriptures, rather as God reveals himself over the long history of the bible people have grappled with the immensity of understanding who he is. Paul's letter to the Romans clearly demonstrates God's faithfulness in that he continues to allow us the

THE CHARACTERISTICS OF FORGIVENESS

freedom to choose what is good or sinful. Of course, there are consequences to choosing sinful acts and Paul outlines what that looks like but that's not because of faithlessness in God, rather faithlessness in us. In no way is Paul saying God abandons us and is never ready to welcome us back. Repentance always leads back to a Father waiting with open arms.

So how does Jesus demonstrate God is faithful? Look at what he says in Matthew 28:20. After Jesus rises from the dead he tells his disciples go into the world and declare the Gospel message to its furthest corners. In order to make sure they knew he would always be with them the very last words we read in the Gospel of Matthew are these: "I am with you always, to the end of the age." How can we ever believe God is not with us after Christ reveals such comforting sentiments! He is always with us, never leaving us, and constantly present to us. He is very interested in our lives and will be with us until the end of time. The author of Hebrews declares to the early church Christ's promise when he writes in chapter 13 verse five, "Keep your lives free from the love of money, and be content with what you have; for he has said, "I will never leave you or forsake you." I think we can say with confidence Jesus Christ does not reveal a God who sleeps, forgets about us, or is uninterested in our lives, but rather a God who is ever present waiting for us to turn to Him and be comforted by his presence.

Of course, given the topic of this book, we cannot ignore the forgiving nature of Christ. This whole book speaks to the fact at the core of Jesus' mission is the act of extending forgiveness to those who will receive him. Through this act of forgiveness Jesus reconciles those who enter into a relationship with him to God and one another. The whole New Testament speaks to this characteristic of Christ. Here are three obvious scripture passages making this very point: Ephesians 1:7 "In him we have redemption through his blood, the forgiveness of our trespasses, according to the riches of his grace." And in Matthew 26:28 we read, "for this is my blood of the covenant, which is poured out for many for the forgiveness of sins." In John 8:10–11 scripture states, "Jesus straightened up and said to her, "Woman, where are they? Has no one condemned you?" She said, "No one, sir." And Jesus said, "Neither do I condemn you. Go your way, and from now on do not sin again."

These three passages echo the very heart of the forgiving nature of Jesus, which of course demonstrates God's forgiving nature. His sacrifice becomes the means for our forgiveness and reconciliation with God. His forgiving nature is so all encompassing we can place ourselves in the shoes of the women caught in adultery and feel his love when he says to us, "Neither do I condemn you." God forgives us of everything we've done, left undone, said or left unsaid and there is nothing we can do to keep him from doing so because there's nothing we can do to keep him from loving us. That's a powerful message and the shame of it is too often we cannot accept it. Because this type of forgiveness is so unbelievable we have difficulty accepting God can really be that way. Maybe that's why the Old Testament is permeated with the idea of offering sacrifice and propitiating God over and over again. It was too difficult for those who had not seen the face of Christ to believe God could love and forgive unconditionally. All we have to do is accept it. Yet, one cannot read the New Testament and find anywhere in Jesus' message a request to do something in order to receive his forgiveness and love. I should clarify that statement, there is one thing we need to do and that's believe, have faith, and accept it. That's what it means to be saved by grace. That's how we know God is all forgiving.

The fifth characteristic revealed through the person of Christ is the just nature of God. People often think of Jesus as a "softie" or a "pushover" forgiving everyone and showing them love without any regard to the pain their hurtful acts have caused. We have softened the image of Christ so much that there's simply no justice in what he does, only forgiveness. Yet, a review of the Scriptures demonstrates otherwise. For example, no one can read the parable of the sheep and goats without recognizing when judgment comes, it's just, swift, and delivered with authority. The parable is found in Matthew 25:31–46:

> When the Son of Man comes in his glory, and all the angels with him, he will sit on his glorious throne. All the

nations will be gathered before him, and he will separate the people one from another as a shepherd separates the sheep from the goats. He will put the sheep on his right and the goats on his left. "Then the King will say to those on his right, 'Come, you who are blessed by my Father; take your inheritance, the kingdom prepared for you since the creation of the world. For I was hungry and you gave me something to eat, I was thirsty and you gave me something to drink, I was a stranger and you invited me in, I needed clothes and you clothed me, I was sick and you looked after me, I was in prison and you came to visit me.' "Then the righteous will answer him, 'Lord, when did we see you hungry and feed you, or thirsty and give you something to drink? When did we see you a stranger and invite you in, or needing clothes and clothe you? When did we see you sick or in prison and go to visit you?' "The King will reply, 'Truly I tell you, whatever you did for one of the least of these brothers and sisters of mine, you did for me.' "Then he will say to those on his left, 'Depart from me, you who are cursed, into the eternal fire prepared for the devil and his angels. For I was hungry and you gave me nothing to eat, I was thirsty and you gave me nothing to drink, I was a stranger and you did not invite me in, I needed clothes and you did not clothe me, I was sick and in prison and you did not look after me.' "They also will answer, 'Lord, when did we see you hungry or thirsty or a stranger or needing clothes or sick or in prison, and did not help you?' "He will reply, 'Truly I tell you, whatever you did not do for one of the least of these, you did not do for me.' "Then they will go away to eternal punishment, but the righteous to eternal life."

We should never confuse the patience of the Lord as a pass for avoiding his just judgment of sin in our lives (Psalm 103:8; 1 Cor 13:4; 1 Tim 1:16). Forgiveness doesn't ignore Justice, but is tempered with mercy. As noted previously, God balances justice, mercy, patience, and all the other important aspects of dealing with sinners perfectly, we distort it.

As we describe each of these characteristics, we find a multitude of evidence demonstrating God's just nature revealed in Jesus

Christ. Scripture speaks of Jesus as the righteous judge of the living and the dead (John 5:22–29) and helps us understand His commandment to treat one another justly (Matthew 7:12). I believe we are correct to say we have a just God who judges justly and it's important we don't confuse His mercy as a "pass" on punishment for sin.

Another characteristic Jesus reveals is the generosity of God. God's first generous act is found in the book of Genesis when he creates the world. He delights in the creative act found in the first chapter of Genesis. He gives life abundantly to plants, animals and ultimately human beings. Jesus' generosity is reflected in this same life-giving act. One of my favorite passages demonstrating the overabundance Jesus offers humanity is when he feeds the multitude as described in Matthew 14:19–20: " And he directed the people to sit down on the grass. Taking the five loaves and the two fish and looking up to heaven, he gave thanks and broke the loaves. Then he gave them to the disciples, and the disciples gave them to the people. They all ate and were satisfied, and the disciples picked up twelve basketfuls of broken pieces that were left over." Remember, right before this His disciples came and said, "You better tell these folks to go off and fend for themselves, it's getting late and they need something to eat." In a sense they were saying to Jesus, "We're not responsible for feeding these people, we don't have enough to share with them and we need what we have for ourselves." Jesus, knowing the hearts of his disciples is keenly aware they are struggling to be hospitable, generous, and trusting in God's willingness to provide. In verse 16 Jesus tells them to feed the people themselves and they immediately respond with, "We only have five loaves and two fish, we can't do it." Then, in his abundant generosity Jesus takes the bread and the fish and performs a miracle. In his abundance, Jesus gives so much for the crowds to eat there are twelve baskets left over. Jesus is generous.

The generosity of Jesus is not just in what he provides but also in what he is willing to give up. Jesus, the Son of God, suspends many of His divine attributes to take on human flesh and dwell among sinners. He lovingly offers himself to God the Father as the instrument of our salvation. Paul recognizes this generous act when he writes to the Philippians using the words from this ancient Christian hymn (Philippians 2:5–8): "Who, being in very nature God, did not consider equality with God something to be used to his own advantage; rather, he made himself nothing by taking the very nature of a servant, being made in human likeness. And being found in appearance as a man, he humbled himself by becoming obedient to death—even death on a cross!"

We can see God's generosity clearly made known in the person of Christ in two distinct ways. First, we recognize his generosity in what he gives us through his abundant grace. Additionally, we benefit from the generosity of God by what he is willing to give up for us. Christ suspended his divinity in order to walk with us, live with us, and die as one of us for the forgiveness of our sins. We might argue from these two simple passages of scripture God is holistically forgiving in ways we struggle to imitate.

The last two characteristics I'm going to explore related to our topic and revealed in Christ are His holiness and compassion. In the book of Acts there are numerous examples of the early Christians recognizing Christ as holy and Lord over all (Acts 2:36; Acts 4:12). Very early after his resurrection the disciples understood Jesus was not just a prophet rather they understood he was God. In fact, they were probably clued into this fact when they walked with him in his earthly ministry but couldn't fully appreciate it until he rose from the dead. An example of their early clue into Christ's holy nature is found in Mark. Mark records the disciples hearing demons call Jesus holy. In Mark chapter one verse 24 Jesus is exorcising a demon who says to him, "What have you to do with us, Jesus of Nazareth? Have you come to destroy us? I know who you are, the Holy One of God." It's clear Jesus is holy and even the demons can't help but proclaim it so.

Along with all the other characteristics revealed in Christ the compassionate nature of God resonates deeply with the human heart. To be compassionate is to "suffer with", and the Christian God is one who doesn't stand far off taking joy in seeing human beings suffer, rather he takes on human flesh and suffers with them. In Mark 1:40-42 Jesus is "Moved with pity" (Some translate pity as compassion) and heals the leper, he tells all those burdened with life's toil to come and rest in him (Matthew 11:28-30) and the burden he gives them to carry is light. One of my favorite examples of Jesus' compassion is found in Luke 7:11-14:

> He went to a town called Nain, and his disciples and a large crowd went with him. As he approached the gate of the town, a man who had died was being carried out. He was his mother's only son, and she was a widow; and with her was a large crowd from the town. When the Lord saw her, he had compassion for her and said to her, "Do not weep." Then he came forward and touched the bier, and the bearers stood still. And he said, "Young man, I say to you, rise!"

Jesus recognized this poor mother's tears for everything they represent. He understood the pain in her soul and appreciated the social ramifications of being a woman with no husband or children to care for her. Even His ability to view human life from an eternal perspective didn't stop him from caring for the temporal needs of people. He had compassion because he was suffering with her in the broken fallen world of first century Palestine.

We need to be acutely aware we can know something about the character of God because God has revealed himself in the person of Jesus Christ. While it may seem the God of the Old Testament contradicts himself in different books of the bible, in Christ we discover they converge presenting themselves in a way that allows us to truly know the Father. Since to know the Son is to know the Father, our experience and record of the character of Jesus provides us with insight into the character of God the Father. Developing a vocation of forgiveness reflective of God's life in us requires possessing an accurate God image as a reference point. We develop a healthy God image by exploring who Jesus is in the scriptures and allowing ourselves to experience Christ as a living person with whom we enter into a relationship. This cannot remain intellectual it must become an emotional experience. Hopefully I have provided you with some core characteristics to guide your understanding of Jesus as part of this process of developing a solid God image. We must experience God as loving, patient, faithful, forgiving, just, generous, holy, and compassionate. These can't just be intellectual concepts about Christ, they need to be experiences we have of God. If we can know God in this way we can develop a sense of our own forgiveness and experience of his love leading us to love and forgive others in this uniquely Christian way. A clear and accurate God image empowers us to love in a biblical Christian way leading us to become people creating atmospheres of love and forgiveness.

Why is it important we develop a healthy God image in our vocation of forgiveness? As noted above, the God image impacts a number of ways in which we think about ourselves and other people. A healthy God image is associated with a number of things important to our topic. Remember, the God image works somewhat unconsciously so it informs that "gut" reaction we have toward others and ourselves in different circumstances. If God is characterized as punitive forgiving others (or yourself) won't come easily because our first reaction is to seek justice and punishment for what we believe is unjust. If we characterize God as overly loving our first reaction toward hurtful individuals might be to overlook the damage their behaviors caused to the relationship and leave open wounds where healing is needed. If our God image reflects a hyper-rational God we look for logical explanations for behaviors before we can forgive them for what they've done. The point I'm trying to make is that an unhealthy God image creates an unhealthy preconscious drive concerning how to exercise the vocation of forgiveness. The Christian needs to form a healthy God image, one congruent with the characteristics outlined above from the scriptures. By meditating on the person of Christ as revealed in the bible it's possible to form a more accurate God image. I urge you to spend a great deal of time reading through the New Testament to understand who Jesus Christ is. By knowing him you can know the true character of God thus forming your God image more accurately. When you have a well formed God image, you understand the generous giver of the free gift of forgiveness.

FORGIVENESS IS NOT RECONCILIATION

Forgiveness is not reconciliation. We often confuse the two because they're so closely related, but one is definitely not the other. I can easily demonstrate this with a story about Janice, one of my past clients. Janice was estranged from her mother. For ten years Janice had no interactions with her. Janice's mother was an alcoholic and emotionally abusive toward her children. Janice was emotionally scarred from her upbringing and often the pain she carried in her heart impacted her relationship with her husband and children. She wanted a better life so she came to me for therapy. She started attending church about the same time we started our sessions. This was a helpful experience and gave her spiritual nourishment as well as connected her with some solid Christian people. She made friends and developed relationships with some mature women in the congregation giving her support and guidance in ways her mother never could. As much as she enjoyed her church experience she always cringed when the pastor spoke about obeying, respecting, and loving your parents. This is a common experience for people struggling with parental relationships in the church. Christians believe God wants them to respect, love, and support their parents yet for some people mothers and fathers are the most destructive people in their lives. The message they hear from the pulpit just doesn't match their experience of growing up in abusive homes. Janice needed to forgive her mother so she could move forward in loving relationships with other people. She needed to break the chains keeping her trapped in past experiences so she could experience the freedom Christ offers her in the present new loving relationships she established. If she could forgive her mother, she might not only experience peace but recognize her mother as the wounded soul she was. Yet Janice believed the word forgiveness meant reconciliation. Janice needed to understand forgiveness was the first step for healing but it didn't mean she had to allow her mother to reenter her life. Forgiveness is something we have to do; reconciliation is something we might do if both parties can come to that place in their broken relationship.

Forgiveness is a choice we make. It depends on nothing more than our own willingness to extend love and good will to someone who hurt us. It's a gift freely given whether received or not by the one we are forgiving. In this book, we are talking about the vocation to forgive those who hurt us because it's what Christ commands. Reconciliation occurs when two people in a broken relationship forgive one another, set the difficult past aside, and begin anew. Janice was not going to reconcile with her mother. Her mother didn't want it, constantly blamed Janice for the problems in the relationship, and continued in her abusive destructive behavior. The only option available to Janice was to sever the relationship with her mother so she could flourish as a mother and wife herself. Yet, this young woman still had the Christian obligation to forgive her mother for what she had done. Using a number of theological and psychological resources I walked Janice through the process of forgiveness and she has been able to find joy and peace in her relationship with her husband and her children. She still struggles with it at times, but she knows it's what Christ asks and discovered it benefits her spiritual, emotional, physical, mental, and relational life. She hopes one day, when her mother is willing to extend love and forgiveness toward her, that reconciliation can occur. Sometimes it must be left to the powers of heaven to shape the relationship in the next life yet sometimes God's grace touches two hearts in this life and a relationship can be restored. For this life the vocation is to forgive. We must be forgiving people because by doing so we make room for the kingdom of God to break its way into this fallen world. Remember, forgiveness is not reconciliation and in this book our focus will be on forgiving those who hurt us, not necessarily facilitating reconciliation to restore the relationship.

SUMMARY OF CHAPTER 2

This chapter's purpose is to help the reader understand the nature and character of forgiveness. We need to understand forgiveness so we understand what it is we're asked to share with other people. Forgiveness is a grace filled act. As noted above it doesn't come naturally for us when we've been hurt or treated unjustly, rather our natural response is to hurt someone back. Forgiveness is an act of grace offered to others because it's been offered to us when we didn't deserve it.

The second point made in this chapter is that forgiveness is a command of God. Just as we're compelled to love one another, we're compelled to forgive one another. Christ requires his followers to be forgiving because it's the key instrument used to renew the earth and allow heaven to break forth into our fallen condition. When we're capable of forgiveness we're capable of healing the wounds hate and anger create. At a bare minimum, we can stop hate and anger from perpetuating itself over and over again from one generation to another.

A third point I wanted to make is that forgiveness has a paradoxical nature to it like most other spiritual practices. Scripture tells us we are forgiven as much as we forgive others. Yet, we don't want to mechanize this concept believing God is a type of vending machine we get something from by putting something in. God reminds us we can only understand and feel his forgiving love if we open ourselves up to the experience of extending it to others. God is always ready to forgive with an overabundance of love; we simply need to be tuned into this forgiving experience by extending it to others. We will know God's forgiveness more perfectly when we give it away to others because he is always ready to pour more of it into our hearts.

Important for extending forgiveness to others is knowing forgiveness is a gift given by a great "gift giving" God. Key to knowing God as generous, loving, sharing, etc. is knowing the characteristics of God. These characteristics shape our God image, an unconscious representation we carry around in our minds regarding the nature of the divine. Living in a sinful world and experiencing sinful acts from others, particularly authority figures such as parents, employers, or ministers of the Gospel, can negatively shape how we view God. If we have a poor image of God in our mind we might have difficulty extending love and forgiveness to others and ourselves. We can correct that poor God image by coming to know God as he truly is. While it may appear the scriptures speak of a schizophrenic God, one who is vengeful and loving at the same time, in their description of the person of Jesus Christ the Christian finds a full and accurate understanding of God. By exploring the New Testament we can be assured God is loving, patient, faithful, forgiving, just, generous, and compassionate! The Christian knows Christ reveals the Father therefore what we read about Jesus Christ in the New Testament is a true reflection of the nature of God. Our God image matters because when it's congruent with the true characteristics of God we are able to love and forgive as God truly wants. Otherwise we are limited by our distorted experience of the nature of God.

The last point made in this chapter reminds us forgiveness is something very different from reconciliation. While reconciliation is indeed a wonderful experience for ending broken relationships, it's not the same thing as forgiveness. Forgiveness is an individual's act of extending love and goodwill toward another. Reconciliation takes two people who choose to forgive, love, and begin anew to reestablish a relationship. Forgiveness is that first step we all need to take if reconciliation will ever be possible.

At this point we've come to a place allowing us to explore how the Christian vocation of forgiveness is lived among the Christian faithful. I am a firm believer that after the scriptures one needs to explore the early Christians writings to get a fuller experience of how the Christian life is lived. These men and women walked in the shadow of Christ, and after his resurrection, the apostles and their followers as well. In a sense, they experienced the "Purest press of the olive." Anyone that loves olive oil knows the first press is where we get the purest oil. These early communities exercised the vocation of forgiveness while being martyred, persecuted, and tested in so many ways. Because of that, I will spend some time in the next chapter exploring their experience of the vocation to forgive.

3

Forgiveness in the Early Christian Community

WE CAN ONLY IMAGINE what it was like to live and worship in the early Christian community. Today's church experience involves Sunday morning church attendance and then a return to our isolated lives disconnected from fellow church members. If we're lucky we fellowship throughout the week, but often our interactions are nothing more than cordial niceties greeting one another and asking about each other's health. It's a far cry from the early Christians' experience of life and worship. Even in intimate settings like the home church I pastor there's a lack of closeness ancient believers experienced within their communities. There are two very strong images used to describe the early Christian church. The first image is that of a close family with ties deeper than those found in biological families. In fact, these early Christians believed they were sons and daughters of God making them brothers and sisters to one another in a very profound way. The second image early Christians used to describe their communities can be found in the New Testament writings of Paul. Paul often referred to the church as the body of Christ. Early Christian writers drew on this image frequently to describe their connection to one another. They experienced such strong interpersonal connectivity that if one person suffered the whole community felt their pain. These early Christians believed if one of them hurt the whole community should come to that individual's aid. When you view yourself as a family of brothers and sisters forgiveness is important for maintaining the strong family bonds forged in communal life. Likewise, thinking of yourself as part of a body means wounds need healed or else they impact the whole organism. Forgiveness is the healing process for both the family and the body.

A very good picture of the early Christian community can be found in the book of Acts. In Acts chapter two we read the following:

> They devoted themselves to the apostles' teaching and fellowship, to the breaking of bread and prayers. Awe came upon everyone, because many wonders and signs were being done by the apostles. All who believed were together and had all things in common; they would sell their possessions and goods and distribute the proceeds to all, as any had need. Day by day, as they spent much time together in the temple, they broke bread at home and ate their food with glad and generous hearts, praising God and having the goodwill of all the people. And day by day the Lord added to their number those who were being saved.

This passage includes a number of points demonstrating the early church's strong sense of community. First, they lived in awe of the great wonders and signs God performed among them. Their closeness to one another, commitment to God, and desire to know Jesus allowed them to experience magnificent miracles. This community had only one agenda item, to remain united in the worship of God and service to one another. There was no church building to construct, no Sunday distraction to draw them away from each other, and no church board meeting to plan. They gathered together because they encountered the living Christ and felt an intrinsic unity because of their common relationship to him. This sense of mission created awe among them and the expectation that Christ would continue to act in their midst. They shared in the Eucharist (The breaking of bread), Scriptures, and prayers continually.

In fact, they didn't just show up for Sunday worship, they were "devoted to the apostles' teaching, fellowship, and the breaking of bread and prayers." Devoted means intensely invested in the things pointing to Christ.

This passage also tells us the early Christians held all things in common. They sold the fruits of their old life to sow a new life among other believers. No one needed anything and much of their time together was spent in prayer and worship as well as the breaking of bread. They were living in this world in a way reflective of how Christians will live in the next. Most important for our discussion is recognizing how intimately connected they were. Their lives depended on this intimate communal experience. Christ built them up into a new temple (Ephesians 2:19–21) where a sacrifice of praise and worship was perpetually offered to God the Father. This intimate connection needed a way to heal when fractures occurred, and that way is the exercise of forgiveness.

This ideal Christian community seems like a dream today. It feels like a distant fantasy because many of our communities are no longer grounded in the person of Jesus Christ. Remember, these Christians lived as they did because Christ was a vivid reality and many of them actually walked with him and encountered him after his resurrection. If our communities aren't centered on Christ we've made other agenda items the reason for our existence. Churches don't intentionally choose to make this shift but when they do their communal focus turns away from encountering Christ to becoming obsessed with buildings and new social ministry programs. Christ has to be the center of our community's mission and vision. In fact, it's because Christ is the center we become brothers and sisters to one another. While Christ's Sonship to the Father is unique, it's through him we become adopted children of God (John 1:12). It's this familial relationship so evident to the first Christians that we've lost. I want to start our exploration of the early Christian experience of forgiveness by looking at how early Christians lived and viewed themselves so we can see how forgiveness is the glue that kept them together.

THE EARLY CHRISTIAN LIFE AS A NEW FAMILY

Christians lived radically different than their contemporaries in the first century. Tertullian, a first century Christian himself noted this when he wrote: "It is mainly the deeds of a love so noble that lead many to put a brand upon us. "See", they say, "how they love one another!" . . . and they are wroth with us, too, because we call each other brethren." [1] First century Romans struggled to understand how a group of strangers could love and care for each other in a way reserved for blood relatives. These early Christians understood accepting a living relationship with Christ meant their old life died. When rising from the baptismal waters they were born again into a new family. They experienced a transformation that not only changed the core of who they were but also their relationships. This transformation of self and relationships was directly related to the radically new life received from the new relationship experienced with Christ. What is often called the "Baptismal bond" supersedes all other bonds. With this new life husband and wife are more than spouses; they are brother and sister as well. Father, son, mother, daughter, grandfather, and grandchildren are all relationships taking second place to the fact believers are members of the family of God. Because of this, Christians lived very differently from the rest of the world. In the ancient world family ties and commitments to ancient clans, classes, and institutions required complete obedience. The Christian experience was very different. Those previous loyalties no longer were defining relationships in the Christian's life. The new Christian was primarily defined by his or her relationship to Jesus Christ and the family of believers called the church. In fact, many who became Christian were disowned by their families and needed their new family to support them and embrace them with radical love; the kind of love Tertullian notes distressed the surrounding culture.

Aristides, a Greek philosopher and second century Christian wrote a beautiful description of how Christians lived differently from those around them. Below is a section of that work in which

---

1. Tertulian *Ante-Nicene Fathers volume* 3 "Apology," 46

you get a sense of this new familial love Christians shared with one another:

> The Christians, O king, while they went about and made search, have found the truth; and as we learned from their writings, they have come nearer to truth and genuine knowledge than the rest of the nations. For they know and trust in God, the Creator of heaven and of earth, in whom and from whom are all things.... Wherefore, they do not commit adultery nor fornication, nor bear false witness, nor embezzle what is held in pledge, nor covet that what is not theirs. They honor father and mother and show kindness to those near to them; and whenever they are judges, they judge uprightly. They do not worship idols made in the image of man; and whatsoever they would not that others should do unto them, they do not do to others; and of the food which is consecrated to idols, they do not eat, for they are pure. And their oppressors they appease (lit: comfort) and make them their friends; they do good to their enemies; and their women, O king, are pure as virgins, and their daughters are modest; and their men keep themselves from every unlawful union and from all uncleanness, in hope of a recompense to come in the other world. Further, if one or other of them have bondmen and bondwomen or children, through love towards them they persuade them to become Christians, and when they have done so, they call them brethren without distinction. They do not worship strange gods, and they go their way in all modesty and cheerfulness. Falsehood is not found among them, and they love one another, and from widows they do not turn away their esteem; and they deliver the orphan from him who treats him harshly. And he, who has, gives to him who has not, without boasting. And when they see a stranger, they take him into their homes and rejoice over him as a very brother; for they do not call them brethren after the flesh, but brethren after the spirit and in God. And whenever one of their poor passes from the world, each one of them according to his ability gives heed to him and carefully sees to his burial. And if they hear that one of their number is imprisoned or afflicted

> on account of the name of their Messiah, all of them anxiously minister to his necessity, and if it is possible to redeem him, they set him free. And if there is among them any that is poor and needy, and if they have no spare food, they fast two or three days in order to supply to the needy their lack of food. They observe the precepts of their Messiah with much care, living justly and soberly as the Lord their God commanded them. Every morning and every hour they give thanks and praise to God for His loving-kindness toward them; and for their food and their drink they offer thanksgiving to him. And if any righteous man among them passes from the world, they rejoice and offer thanks to God; and they escort the body as if he were setting out from one place to another near. And when a child has been born to one of them, they give thanks to God. [2]

This is a powerful description of what it meant to live as a Christian in the first century. You can also gather from its reading how deeply they understood themselves to be members of a new family. They called one another brother and sister, mother and father. They lived a life so foreign to the culture it must have seemed heaven fell from the sky and planted itself within the boundaries of the Roman Empire. To be a Christian was to be a member of a new family with God as Father.

Another early Christian writer captured this familial experience in his attempt to explain the Christian faith to authority figures. Athenagoras who wrote an apology presented to Emperors Marcus Aurelius and Commodus about A.D. 177 had this to say about the Christian communal experience:

> On this account, too, according to age, we recognize some as sons and daughters, others we regard as brothers and sisters, and to the more advanced in life we give the honor due to fathers and mothers. On behalf of those, then, to whom we apply the names of brothers and sisters, and other designations of relationship, we exercise

---

2. Aristides *Ante-Nicene Fathers volume* 9 "The Apology of Aristides, " 276–277

the greatest care so that their bodies should remain undefiled and uncorrupted.[3]

It's obvious the early Christian community understood themselves to be a newly created family. New believers saw in their fellow Christians a deep bond established because of their new life in Christ. You can find examples of this new understanding of fellow Christians in the bible. First Timothy 5:1–2 states, "Do not rebuke an older man but encourage him as you would a father, younger men as brothers, older women as mothers, younger women as sisters, in all purity." More importantly, Christ himself demonstrates being a believer means having radically new relationships with him and the community of faith. Recall the story from the bible when Christ is told his mother and brothers are looking for him. Matthew tells us Jesus responded in the following way: "Who is my mother? And who are my brothers? And he stretched out his hand toward his disciples and said 'Behold, my mother and my brethren! For whoever does the will of my Father who is in heaven, this is my brother, sister, and mother." At this point you're wondering how this discussion relates to forgiveness. I will answer that shortly, but I want to explore another image of the Christian community demonstrating the close ties they shared so we can further understand the healing nature of forgiveness.

THE EARLY CHRISTIAN COMMUNITY—THE BODY OF CHRIST

One cannot possibly have read the letters of Paul or sung any early Christian hymn and not heard somehow Christians understood themselves to be the body of Christ. For example, in Paul's letter to the Romans Chapter 12 verse 5 we read, "so we, who are many, are one body in Christ, and individually we are members one of another." In other letters Paul continues the same theme. Take the following passage from 1st Corinthians 12:12–31:

---

3. Athenagoras *Ante-Nicene Fathers* volume 2 "A Plea for Christians," 146

> For just as the body is one and has many members, and all the members of the body, though many, are one body, so it is with Christ. For in the one Spirit we were all baptized into one body—Jews or Greeks, slaves or free—and we were all made to drink of one Spirit. Indeed, the body does not consist of one member but of many. If the foot would say, "Because I am not a hand, I do not belong to the body," that would not make it any less a part of the body. And if the ear would say, "Because I am not an eye, I do not belong to the body," that would not make it any less a part of the body. If the whole body were an eye, where would the hearing be? If the whole body were hearing, where would the sense of smell be? But as it is, God arranged the members in the body, each one of them, as he chose. If all were a single member, where would the body be? As it is, there are many members, yet one body. The eye cannot say to the hand, "I have no need of you," nor again the head to the feet, "I have no need of you." On the contrary, the members of the body that seem to be weaker are indispensable, and those members of the body that we think less honorable we clothe with greater honor, and our less respectable members are treated with greater respect; whereas our more respectable members do not need this. But God has so arranged the body, giving the greater honor to the inferior member, that there may be no dissension within the body, but the members may have the same care for one another. If one member suffers, all suffer together with it; if one member is honored, all rejoice together with it. Now you are the body of Christ and individually members of it. And God has appointed in the church first apostles, second prophets, third teachers; then deeds of power, then gifts of healing, forms of assistance, forms of leadership, various kinds of tongues. Are all apostles? Are all prophets? Are all teachers? Do all work miracles? Do all possess gifts of healing? Do all speak in tongues? Do all interpret? But strive for the greater gifts. And I will show you a still more excellent way.

And again we read in Colossians 3:14: "Above all, clothe yourselves with love, which binds everything together in perfect harmony.

And let the peace of Christ rule in your hearts, to which indeed you were called in the one body. "There are many more references in Paul's letters regarding this body imagery indicating the early church saw themselves as more than a gathering of people or a tight family but something almost "mystical." They saw themselves as a mysteriously united body with Christ as its head (Colossians 1:18; 1 Corinthians 12:27). Clement, in 150 AD wrote, "so then, let us choose to be of the church of life, so that we may be saved. I do not, however, suppose ye are ignorant that the living Church is the body of Christ." [4] His words continue in the tradition of Paul.

Another first century author who wrote an allegorical work entitled *The Shepherd* says this; "So also they who have believed on the Lord through His Son, and are clothed with these spirits, shall become one spirit, one body, and the colour of their garments shall be one." [5] One of my favorite descriptions of this new mystical body comes from Origin. Origin lived from 185 to 255 AD and is considered the father of Christian theology. In one of his writings he says this about the church:

> We say that the Holy Scriptures declare the body of Christ, animated by the Son of God, to be the whole church of God, and the members of this body—considered as a whole—consist of those who are believers ... The Word, arousing and moving the whole body, the church, to befitting action, awakens, moreover, each individual member belonging to the church. [6]

This is a beautiful image of the church existing as one body and the Word of God pulsing through it as blood through the human body, animating and giving life to all its members.

Both the familial image and the body image are indicators of the extremely close relationships the people of God shared. Yet, even the early church struggled to maintain these close ties. Christians forgot (and still forget) the vocation we share to be a

---

4. Second Clement *Ante-Nicene Fathers* volume 7 "The Homily Ascribed to Clement," 521

5. Hermas *Ante-Nicene Fathers* volume 2 "The Pastor of Hermas, " 48.

6. Origin *Ante-Nicene Fathers* volume 4 "Origen Against Celsus," 595

uniting force within the church. About the year 250 AD, Cyprian, a Bishop of the church in Carthage North Africa wrote the following because of his concern that this early understanding of how to live in common was fading:

> Then they (Christians) used to give for sale houses and estates; and that they might lay up for themselves treasures in heaven, presented to the apostles the price of them, to be distributed for the use of the poor. Be now we do not even give the tenths from our patrimony; and while our Lord bids us sell, we rather buy and increase our store. Thus has the vigor of faith dwindled away among us; thus has the strength of believers grown weak. And therefore the Lord, looking to our days, says in His Gospel, "When the Son of man cometh, think you that He shall find faith on the earth? [7]

Early in the church's development the way of life described in the book of acts was beginning to fracture. Paul dealt with issues and divisions in the church (Read both his letters to the Corinthians) but Cyprian was noticing the simple fact communities once drawn closely together were beginning to look more and more like the surrounding communities of Rome.

What do you do when breaks and fractures occur in the community? How does one remedy this situation? There are three distinct ways Christians have historically corrected these problems. First, make Christ the center of communal life. Secondly, foster a life of love and concern for one another, and lastly, become a forgiving community.

THE CENTER OF A COMMUNITY—CHRIST

Groups of people who gather together frequently are not necessarily a community. Establishing nominal affiliations does not mean a community has developed, particularly in the way early Christians understood themselves to be a community. They took the commandment to love seriously because it was given to them

---

7. Cyprian *Ante-Nicene Fathers volume* 5 "The Treatises of Cyprian," 429

The Christian Vocation of Forgiveness

by Christ, lived and demonstrated in his life, and radically changed the social order among them in a very real way. This radical new sense of community depended on Jesus Christ being the center of everything they did.

Jesus was the center of early Christian communal life first and foremost in how he was worshipped. They gathered together weekly and encountered Christ in two distinct ways. The first was through his Word where Christ was proclaimed and experienced through the writings of the Old and New Testament. In the Old Testament, the prophets and the law spoke of a coming messiah who would change the world. In the Old Testament, the early Christians saw a prefigured Christ within the text. In biblical theology, this is called typology, but one does not need to be a scripture scholar to recognize how the early Christians understood Jesus Christ as the key for understanding God's unfolding revelation from creation to his birth. The Old Testament gives us a sense of the coming redemption of God found in the New Testament's account of Christ's life. Augustine of Hippo describes it this way: "This grace hid itself under a veil in the Old Testament, but it has been revealed in the New Testament according to the most perfectly ordered dispensation of the ages, forasmuch as God knew how to dispose all things."[8]

Christ is the center of all scripture, and evidence of this is found in his own teaching to the early Christian community in the Gospel of John. In the Gospel Jesus says to the Pharisees: "You search the Scriptures because you think that in them you have eternal life; it is these that testify about Me; and you are unwilling to come to Me so that you may have life" (John 5:39, 40). Other biblical passages make the same point. These are found in Luke 24:13–27, 44–48; I Corinthians 1:22–23; 2:2, and 2 Corinthians 4:5. In the scriptures, both Old and New, Jesus is the center and key to their understanding. Early Christians knew this and centered their lives on hearing scripture at their weekly gatherings

---

8. This comes from Augustine's writings against the Pelagians. Pelagians were a sect of Christians who believed original sin did not impact human nature's ability to choose between good and evil without Divine assistance (i.e. grace).

to discover Christ in their midst. Recollecting these stories and teachings mystically made Christ present among them.

The second way Christ was central in their weekly worship was through the celebration of Eucharist. In the blessing and breaking of bread the early Christian community believed Christ was present to feed them and transform them. Paul demonstrates how seriously early Christians were about participating in the Eucharist in 1st Corinthians 11:23-27

> For I received from the Lord that which I also delivered to you: that the Lord Jesus on the same night in which He was betrayed took bread; and when He had given thanks, He broke it and said, "Take, eat; this is My body which is broken for you; do this in remembrance of Me." In the same manner He also took the cup after supper, saying, "This cup is the new covenant in My blood. This do, as often as you drink it, in remembrance of Me." For as often as you eat this bread and drink this cup, you proclaim the Lord's death till He comes. Therefore whoever eats this bread or drinks this cup of the Lord in an unworthy manner will be guilty of the body and blood of the Lord.

Paul reminds the early Christian community the importance of Eucharist and that it's an act in which the Lord himself is encountered. He feeds them with his body and blood and the community is united in Christ, their center. Christ, the very head of this body, is broken and shared among them. In fact, this mystical encounter is so special Paul reminds Christians if they participate in it unworthily, they condemn themselves. Whatever your position is regarding "how" Christ is encountered in the Eucharist, one cannot deny he "is" encountered and that's what mattered most to the early Christian community. In the midst of their weekly worship, they encountered Christ in his Word and in the Eucharist. The centrality of Christ in the communal life was essential.

The third way early Christians encountered Christ was in one another. We read in Matthew our efforts to relieve the suffering of others are a way to relieve the suffering of Christ. We are challenged to recognize Christ in our fellow human beings (Matthew

The Christian Vocation of Forgiveness

25:40). In Paul's conversion to Christianity he's chastised by the Lord while persecuting Christians for the very fact when he's persecuting them, Paul's persecuting Christ (Acts 9:4). When Paul is knocked to the ground Christ asks him, "Why are you persecuting me?" Christ doesn't ask Paul why he's persecuting "them" he asks why Paul is persecuting "me" (Christ himself). This deep recognition that Christ is found in each Christian was important for the early Christian community. It was part of the fabric making them intimately connected to one another.

Christian communities need to center themselves on Christ. The more and more we move away from recognizing Christ as the center of our community the less and less we become a truly Christian gathering. Dietrich Bonhoeffer wrote a book called, *Life Together, A Discussion of Christian Fellowship* that wonderfully describes the need to be centered on Christ to flourish as a healthy Christian community. In it he writes:

> I have community with others and I shall continue to have it only through Jesus Christ. The more genuine and the deeper our community becomes, the more will everything else between us recede, the more clearly and purely will Jesus Christ and his work become the one and only thing that is vital between us. We have one another only through Christ, but through Christ we do have one another, wholly, and for all eternity.[9]

Bonhoeffer's words reflect what the early Christian church understood so well. To truly be a Christian community we need to be Christ centered. It's in Christ our fraternal love finds its source and transforms the relationships we have with one another. Left to our own devices we would surely begin to manipulate one another seeking our own best interests first and foremost before that of others. Community would look like the tribes found on the popular reality show Survivor. Yet with Christ at the center of our worship in Word, Eucharist and in one another, little by little Jesus becomes central to our communal experience. We are transformed into the

---

9. Dietrich Bonhoeffer, *Life Together*, 25–26

body of Christ by allowing scripture, Eucharist, and Christian charity become the ethos of what we do.

Fractures appear in the body of Christ because we forget the very thing we are. When we regain Christ as our center we rediscover who we are. The effect of making Christ our center is a community built on love. If we believe God is love, and to live in love is to live in God (John 4:16) then the Christian community built on incarnational love is built on God.

LIVE IN LOVE—THE BOND OF COMMUNITY

Anyone reading the writings of the early Christians discovers they are a community of intense love. I've already articulated some of this but let me address the idea of love in relation to forgiveness from the perspective of community. First, let's clarify what we mean by the word love because the English language uses the same word in a number of ways. For example, if I talk about loving my new computer in the same way I talk about loving my wife I'd be in big trouble! I also use the same word love to talk about how I feel toward my mother, brother, children, and my favorite food. Every time I say I love something I use the same word. Intuitively we understand these are different forms of love, but if someone from another planet were to read a document written in English about loving God, neighbor, car, wife, etc. they might find it odd human beings had this emotional experience in the same way for these very different things.

In the Greek language, there are four words used to convey the meaning of love. The first is storge, which means to have a natural affection for others. While the word exists in the Greek language, it's not used in the bible so we're not going to spend any time unpacking its meaning. The three words I'm most interested in exploring are eros, philia, and agape. These three words are found in the bible and describe the human experience of love in a very holistic way. By exploring what they mean we can have a better understanding of the type of love forgiveness attempts to restore. Let's start by exploring eros.

The Christian Vocation of Forgiveness

It's important to note the word eros is not used in the New Testament and is only found in the Greek version of the Old Testament (Septuagint) twice. Eros is a passionate romantic type of love. It's the type of love Paris had for Helen in the Iliad and Juliet shares with Romeo. Ancient tragedies are filled with examples of the power and destructive nature of eros love. Because of the consuming destructive nature of eros many ancient philosophers believed it was something to avoid. A good example is found in the work of Lucretius, a Roman poet and philosopher from the first century. He writes the following in his book *On the Nature of Things*:

> Venus should be entirely shunned, for once her darts have wounded men, the sword gains strength and festers by feeding. Day by day the madness grows and the misery becomes heavier. This is the one thing whereof the more we have, the more does our heart burn with the cursed desire. When the gathering desire is sated, the old frenzy is back upon them.

Lucretius recognizes erotic love, as much as we covet it in the 21st century, is a poison making human beings mad feeding upon one another like animals. In fact, this passionate romantic love can become so overwhelming we make it a god of its own and the object of our love an idol to be worshipped. This kind of love can quickly become unhealthy. While it's not necessarily wrong to be passionate about someone, it certainly can become sinful when it consumes us. St. Augustine understood the danger of this type of love left unchecked. He often discusses in his book *The Confessions* his passion for women and his unchecked desire for their beauty and the beauty of created things. He writes the following:

> Too late love I Thee, O Thou Beauty of ancient days, yet ever new! Too late I loved Thee! And behold, Thou wert within, and I abroad, and there I searched for Thee; deformed I, plunging amid those fair forms which Thou hadst made. Thou wert within me, but I was not with thee. Things held me far from Thee, which unless they were in Thee, were not at all. [10]

10. Augustine, *The Confessions*, 253

Another famous line from the same book describes how eros love drew him into an all-consuming sense of sexual pleasure. In the text, he shares one of his frequent prayers, which says, "Give me chastity and continence but not yet."[11] So while eros love has its place, its place is very limited in the Christian life. Additionally, this kind of love can get in the way of a virtuous life because it leads men to be destructive, hateful, and aggressive more often than gentle, humble, and forgiving. For our purposes, the redeeming quality of eros is its ability to drive us toward the object of our passions and when that passion becomes God it's a positive force in our lives. However, when we're passionately drawn toward anything other than God, we sin.

Perhaps God created eros love to passionately draw us toward him but we were meant to experience love more holistically. If love remains in its "eros" state it becomes maddening. Philia is the next dimension of love required for a more holistic experience. C.S. Lewis writes in his book *The Four Loves* the following, "To the Ancients, Friendship seemed the happiest and most fully human of all loves; the crown of life and the school of virtue. The modern world, in comparison, ignores it." [12] I am in agreement with Lewis, it seems the modern world ignores philia love particularly as expressed in the scriptures. For example, the friendship (philia) love between Jonathan and David seems very foreign to us when read by the modern reader. In fact, some modern interpreters describe David and Jonathan's love as homosexual because when reading it you get the sense these men are deeply in love. This of course is not true; this misinterpretation is merely the result of our infrequent exposure to examples of deep friendship love as expressed between David and Jonathan. In our contemporary setting, women are more likely to experience this type of friendship than men. There's a stigma attached to this type of love relationship for men, but women seem to have the blessing of modern society for intimate relationships. Very few men experience philia

---

11. Ibid, 181
12. C.S. Lewis *The Four Loves*, 39

today with other men, yet the early Christian church knew this type of love very well.

Philia transcends family ties and allegiances and unites people in unexpected ways. It creates a relationship from two people's pure consent to love one another. Husbands and wives "should" experience this type of love, as should the church community. Philia is a deep love based in free will. It transcends traditional relationship ties, the length and duration to those relationships, and the manner in which people share values, beliefs, and ideas in a very powerful way.

Jesus demonstrated philia (and all levels of love) for his disciples frequently. Jesus was passionate for us, desiring us with eros love driving him to the cross. Francis Thompson captures this passionate desire in his poem *The Hound of Heaven*. In that poem, God is described as a hound pursuing his prey voraciously until it's captured. Jesus also demonstrates his philia toward his disciples by the very fact he calls us friends. In John 15:15 Jesus says to his disciples: " I do not call you servants any longer, because the servant does not know what the master is doing; but I have called you friends, because I have made known to you everything that I have heard from my Father." A disciple is a friend of God because God has humbled himself to communicate on an intimate level sharing intimate details of his life with his creation. This is a freely chosen act transcending the natural relationship between God and man where man is a servant to God. In this beautiful gift of philia, God establishes a long-lasting relationship with his disciples and initiates a level of intimacy that transcends the master slave relationship and graciously invites the disciples into a relationship marked by friendship. Early Christians recognized because God offers this kind of love to them they must do the same for each other.

Finally, no talk of Christian love is complete without a discussion about agape love. Yes, eros draws us passionately toward that which we love but if left unchecked it leads to idolatry. When tempered with philia, our love becomes one of deep friendship allowing us to recognize the dignity each human person possesses. That which we passionately pursue is appreciated as a person not merely an object to be used for our own ends but loved for the dignity they possess. By experiencing philia love we develop a strong community deeply interested in and connected to one another, but it's agape love that allows someone to go beyond deep intimacy to experience sacrificial love. Agape is used 320 times in the New Testament. Interestingly, the term is more frequently used in reference to how God loves his people rather than how people love one another. This probably happens because agape is a type of love so selfless and sacrificial only God can truly love this way. When people love sacrificially it's only because of God's grace infused in their life. In fact, scripture demonstrates the struggle people have achieving the heights of agape. In the passage where Jesus and Peter discuss whether or not Peter loves the Lord we can see the struggle to understand the love of God. We read in John 21:15–17 the following:

> When they had finished breakfast, Jesus said to Simon Peter, "Simon son of John, do you love me more than these?" He said to him, "Yes, Lord; you know that I love you." Jesus said to him, "Feed my lambs." A second time he said to him, "Simon son of John, do you love me?" He said to him, "Yes, Lord; you know that I love you." Jesus said to him, "Tend my sheep." He said to him the third time, "Simon son of John, do you love me?" Peter felt hurt because he said to him the third time, "Do you love me?" And he said to him, "Lord, you know everything; you know that I love you." Jesus said to him, "Feed my sheep."

From this passage, we get a glimpse of how difficult it is for human beings to understand the love of God. Jesus asks Peter if he loves him. Peter responds he surely does. What we can't see in the English translation is when Jesus ask Peter the first two times if he loves him he uses the word agape. In this way, he's basically asking Peter, do you love me with the sacrificial divine love I have shown you and the other disciples? In all three of Peter's responses back to Christ he uses the Greek word Philia. He just doesn't get what Jesus is asking. In fact, he's a little confused. Jesus asks, "Do you love (Agape) me?" and Peter responds, "I love (Philia) you." Because Jesus wants to teach Peter about Christian love in the form of agape he must go deeper and asks him again using the same word, agape. The last time Jesus asks Peter if he loves him, Jesus changes the vocabulary and uses the word philia. It's as if Jesus knows while Peter doesn't get it yet, he will eventually. Jesus knows the full experience of love Christians are called to display is something we grow into but never completely understand because it's the pure love of God. After the dialogue, Jesus tells Peter one day he will display agape love. He tells Peter there will be a day when you will be led by the waist and taken to a place you won't want to go. Jesus is prophesying to Peter about his death and that one day Peter will show his ultimate love for Christ when he is martyred for his Lord. That will be Peter's agape response.

The early Christian community knew love required more than passion. They discovered it transcends casual friendships and is meant to imitate the love of God. They understood love as the nourishing force within the body of Christ that included each of them as members. Their intimacy for one another had to be holistic expressions of love, not just some casual friendship on Sundays. Together, they had a strong passion to be bound together and seek God above all other things (Eros love). This passion for God meant they would live in a deep brotherly relationship, one transcending natural family ties. They were family regardless of race, bloodline, or social status; they were a new family (Philia love). Ultimately however, they knew they were meant to be living icons of the love of God, a sacrificial love in which their whole existence was poured out for one another (Agape love). Loving holistically as these Christians did meant loving in a way that fostered forgiveness. The body must have a way of healing itself and these early Christians recognized forgiveness as the means for accomplishing this noble task.

SUMMARY OF CHAPTER 3

The purpose of this chapter was to demonstrate the key characteristics allowing early Christians to practice forgiveness in a way we barely comprehend today. Forgiveness requires a number of factors to be a part of a person's life. First, there's a motivation to be radically different, to change one's natural inclination to harm the transgressor. It requires a person to be something that doesn't come naturally. It means becoming more human than animal, more saint than sinner. To have this level of engagement with someone who hurt you requires a disposition of reciprocity. When a person is open to the grace of God and the possibility they can be changed, God will transform them. Key to being able to forgive others is recognizing the individual who hurt you is an individual deserving love. The early Christians recognized the power of love in their lives because Jesus Christ was the incarnation of love. Love is after all the very nature of God. So, the first thing this Christian community taught its followers is God is love and we must love one another because he commands it. In this chapter, we talked about the tight bond of love these communities displayed for one another.

The second most important characteristic these communities displayed to be forgiving communities was their deep sense of empathy for one another. In the first five hundred years, these Christians saw one another as brothers and sisters, as being a part of the same body. They were a family with Christ at their center requiring them to find reasons to connect and live in harmony with one another. They saw each other as human beings plagued by the same diseases, sins, and desires. They understood if someone hurt them it was probably because that individual was hurting and suffering from the ailments of a fallen broken world. Because they understood each other and their world so well, they followed Christ's example absorbing the impact of sin in their brother's or sister's life and instead of perpetuating its effect by hurting someone else, they responded with love and goodwill stopping the awful pattern from repeating itself again. Love, empathy, and the sense they are intimately connected with one another helped them exercise forgiveness.

We have come to a place in the book where we need to explore how we can acquire and exercise forgiveness in our lives. With a solid biblical understanding of why forgiveness is part of our vocation and a sense of how early Christians developed particular characteristics to be forgiving people, we can look at how to apply principles in our lives that allow us to become forgiving people. What I am going to share in the next chapter is some of the research in psychology that outlines how forgiveness is exercised. These practical steps are something Christians can use daily to act in a way reflective of the forgiving nature of God. When merged with the theological ideas presented so far, the Christian has a powerful tool for transforming his or her world, relationships, and life.

4

A Psychological and Theological Look at Forgiveness

UP TO THIS POINT, we've gone through a great deal of material demonstrating why forgiveness matters for those walking in the way of Christ. We've discussed how the early Christians made forgiveness a key part of their communal life simply because experiencing strong relationships required them to forgive each other. In this chapter, I'll outline two psychological theories about forgiveness and connect them to the theological ideas we've already discussed. These models have been refined by psychologists and implemented in a number of therapeutic ways. The models discussed in the following pages have helped many people resolve the pain caused by others because of hurtful acts, words, and intentions. I've used these models to structure my own pastoral and clinical interventions and they inform my own personal practice of forgiveness. Other research exists regarding this topic but most of it points back to the key ideas found in these two seminal models of forgiveness. Therefore, I will summarize both and synthesize their key ideas to provide you with foundational concepts for building practical ways to become a more forgiving person.

CAN WE REALLY FORGIVE OTHERS?

My wife and I were planning our vacation for the summer of 2015. We had the usual stops in mind as we sat down and thought through what we wanted to do. We were headed to Orlando Florida where we stay at a resort with other friends and then we decided to make our way up the east coast back to Virginia Beach. Instead of our usual stop in Hilton Head we decided to stay in Charleston South Carolina and spend time shopping and exploring the city. Little did we know one of the worst acts of racial violence ever experienced in this country would happen right across the street from our hotel. We weren't there when it happened, our trip was planned for July and this violent act occurred in June. However, even after a month's time the result of this evil act profoundly impacted our visit to this historic city. Yes, I'm talking about the shooting that occurred at Mother Emmanuel African Methodist Episcopal Church.

It was a warm June night and like most Wednesday nights at numerous churches across the country people were gathering for prayer and bible study. For years, this gathering was uneventful but on this night a white man named Dylann Roof entered the church and sat quietly pondering his next move. He was welcomed by those in attendance and even claimed because of their kindness he was reconsidering his violent intentions. Unfortunately, the evening didn't end in peace, Dylann pulled out his gun and killed nine people including the pastor Clementa Pinckney. Dylann killed without discrimination in regards to gender or age, he was only interested in killing people because they were black. His disdain for African Americans and feelings of hatred motivated him to pull the trigger on his weapon again and again. Among the dead were Sharonda Coleman-Singleton a 45-year-old mother of three and a high school track coach. Cynthia Hurd age 54, a librarian at the public library for 31 years. Tywanza Sanders, a young 26-year-old graduate of Allen University in Columbia. Tywanza died trying to save his 87-year-old aunt Susie Jackson who was also killed that evening. He told Dylann to shoot him and leave his aunt alone but reports say Dylann said it didn't matter he was going to kill everyone anyway. After he killed Tywanza he eventually shot Susie Jackson. Tywanza was the youngest victim to die that night and his aunt the oldest. This story is beyond tragic and unfortunately not the only of its kind. Think of the many lives lost at the hands of so many terrorist attacks around the world. As I write these very sentences I'm reminded just yesterday, November 13th 2015, terrorists killed and held hostage numerous people in Paris France. Stories of genocide in countries across the globe, murders in local communities, and abuse and neglect in families are not short in supply. The question is, if any of these events happened to you or someone you love could you forgive the perpetrators? The answer has to be yes. Why does it have to be yes? Because if it's no, then we're trapped in a cycle of hatred and self-defeat giving the demons in hell something to celebrate. They rejoice with every act of vengeance and self-loathing that terror and violence inflict on the survivors of trauma. If we can't forgive people, we're forever held captive by the traumatic experiences they've inflicted upon us.

The most moving words of forgiveness I've ever read came from the families of the victims killed that night at Mother Emmanuel African Methodist Episcopal Church. The Washington Post published an article on June 19th by Elahe Izadi called "*The Powerful Words of Forgiveness Delivered to Dylann Roof by Victims' Relatives*" which captured the exemplary Christian spirit of forgiveness this community incarnationally represented to Charleston and the world. Here are some of the things these hurting wounded people had to say to the man who killed those they loved simply because of the color of their skin:

> We welcomed you Wednesday night in our Bible study with welcome arms. You have killed some of the most beautiful people that I know. Every fiber in my body hurts and I'll, I'll never be the same. Tywanza Sanders was my son. But Tywanza Sanders was my hero. Tywanza was my hero. . . . May God have mercy on you.
>
> —Felicia Sanders, mother of Tywanza Sanders

> I forgive you. You took something very precious away from me. I will never get to talk to her ever again. I will never be able to hold her again, but I forgive you, and have mercy on your soul. . . . You hurt me. You hurt a lot of people. If God forgives you, I forgive you.
>
> —Nadine Collier, daughter of victim Ethel Lance

> Although my grandfather and the other victims died at the hands of hate, this is proof, everyone's plea for your soul, is proof that they lived in love and their legacies will live in love. So hate won't win. And I just want to thank the court for making sure that hate doesn't win.
>
> —Wanda Simmons, Granddaughter of victim Daniel Simmons.

If you're like me you hear these words and say to yourself, "I'm not sure I could be that forgiving." I understand. Forgiving someone appears to be a monumental task when someone killed a person you love through a senseless act of violence. But believe me, you can forgive people who do these terrible things. The surviving relatives of these victims aren't superhuman, they're superheroes of forgiveness. These are men and women just like you and me. That's comforting and scary at the same time. It's comforting because it means you and I can choose to be forgiving people. It's scary because it means just like these ordinary people we might find ourselves needing to forgive someone who acted in the same way as Dylann Roof. The important lesson to learn from these brave families is we can be forgiving because forgiveness is a choice. Like love, forgiveness is more about choices than feelings. When we choose to forgive someone, we must learn to behave and think in a particular way that impacts how we feel about the situation. Thinking, feeling, and behaving are intimately connected. I know many of you reading this are saying, "Just choosing to forgive someone doesn't make me feel like I forgave them. Because I don't feel like I've forgiven them I must not be a forgiving person." Yet, this first choice to forgive is indeed an important step in the process. The choice to forgive and then acting in a forgiving way

A PSYCHOLOGICAL AND THEOLOGICAL LOOK AT FORGIVENESS

leads to feelings that come with being a forgiving person. Let me help you understand the psychology behind the process so you can see where this is going.

Think about it this way; you really don't have total control over how you think, feel, and in some ways, behave most days of your life. For example, you may believe you have total control over what you think but if I tell you not to think of the color blue chances are most of you just did simply by reading these words. You also can't really control how you feel. You can't make yourself happy or sad simply because you want to, it's much more complex than giving simple commands to your emotional processing system. Lastly, there are times you behave in a certain way and just can't control it. Addicts know this very well. I'm addicted to chocolate. There are times I tell myself I won't eat any chocolate for a whole day. Yet, I watch myself open the candy drawer, unwrap the candy bar, and as I'm doing it my mind is telling my body, "STOP!" We don't have complete control over these spheres of our life. . . . but we do have some control. We're able to impact how we feel by doing and reflecting on certain things. While we have the most control over what we do (Behavior), we also have some control over how we think, which can then control to some degree how we feel. Thinking, doing, and feeling are intertwined and each impacts the other. If we can impact our behaviors and our thoughts, we might just be able to impact our emotions.

Still not convinced? Try this simple exercise. Sit in your chair, relax, and force yourself to smile. Do that for about 3 minutes. If you've tried it, you'll notice your mood gets slightly elevated. You feel a little happier than you did before the exercise. This is an example of how our most basic physiological behaviors, our physical acts, can impact our mood. Try another exercise. Do the same thing but this time think about the happiest moments of your life. Force yourself to smile and imagine yourself doing something you really enjoy. Did your mood change? It should have at least shifted some, particularly because you added positive cognition to your basic physiological change. Psychologists have been demonstrating this physiological and cognitive connection to emotion for some time. A popular exercise is to take a pen, hold it with your teeth forcing your facial muscles to replicate the same movements you make when you smile. Many people report elevated emotions when they do this for a short period of time. If you hold the pen with your lips (forcing the face to create a type of frown) you will begin to experience sadness.[1] Your physiological behavior impacts your emotions.

How does this relate to our discussion about forgiveness? By choosing to forgive someone you set in motion behaviors and cognitions that lessen your feelings of hurt and anger allowing you to live a life much more capable of doing good things for the Kingdom of God. By choosing to be more than the pain you're experiencing you say to the world God gives us a life so abundant that it's bigger than the sin and evil inflicting us daily. In the next section of this chapter I'm going to share two models of forgiveness that build upon the idea the choice to forgive can reverse the pain and suffering caused by others. What these superheroes of forgiveness demonstrated in the aftermath of the shootings in Charleston is we're not trapped by the evil committed by others, our Christian walk gives witness to something greater than anything they can do.

REACH MODEL OF FORGIVENESS BY EVERETT WORTHINGTON

Everett Worthington is a well-known psychologist and considered an expert in the study of forgiveness. He has done a great deal of research in this area and has a strong publication record regarding the practice and benefits of forgiveness. Worthington came up with an empirically based approach to this subject rooted in the way our bodies react to stress and the "fight or flight" response built into our autonomic nervous system. His basic premise is when we're emotionally hurt and think about that hurt, our physiological reaction is the same as when we're being physically threatened.

1. William Flack Jr., James D. Laird, and Lorraine A. Cavallaro. "Separate and Combined Effects of Facial Expressions and Bodily Postures on Emotional Feelings" *European Journal of Social Psychology*

Our neurological system triggers the fight or flight response setting the stress systems into action that normally help us resolve threatening situations. The stress system allows us to either fight or run from the threat. When we feel as if we can't do either we act out in anger and frustration because we feel trapped. This response becomes conditioned and is triggered by anything reminding us of the person who caused the initial pain. The stress response isn't only psychological but includes biological triggers and responses activated each time we're reminded of what happened. For Worthington, this process can be reversed if one steps through five levels of therapeutic engagement. This process eventually leads us to forgive the person who hurt us and frees us from the emotional trap harboring negative emotions creates. Worthington's model is often referred to as the pyramid model of forgiveness because you move up and down through five levels as you process your anger, frustration, and pain. Let's explore these five levels and discuss the tasks involved in each.

Level 1—Recalling the Hurt

When someone is considering whether or not to forgive another person, Worthington recommends taking the time to reflect in some detail on what caused them to feel the way they do. At this level, it's hoped the client will override the paralyzing and reactionary responses felt every time the painful stimulus is recalled. Worthington identifies the unforgiving response as something similar to a reaction toward objects we fear like a spider, dog, or heights. Yes, anger toward someone who hurt you might be more intense, but for Worthington the physiological reactions are similar. Just as one is conditioned to avoid painful experiences and seek pleasurable ones, being hurt by another person causes us to avoid any thought about the experience and when we can't avoid reexperiencing it we become angry and frustrated. To overcome this conditioned response Worthington believes recalling the event in the appropriate context can begin the process of extinction. Extinction occurs when exposure to something over and over again happens without the associated negative feelings so this association can begin to lessen and the physiological connection dissipate. Here's how he describes it:

> Importantly, repetition of the conditioned stimulus—cognition about the person who inflicted the hurt—without reexperiencing the full depth of pain is crucial. This extinction actually occurs throughout the intervention protocol, but is concentrated in the early stage of intervention. Recalling the hurt involves extinction, which does not eliminate the fear conditioning, but does change the response to the unconditioned stimulus; this is the beginning of forgiveness.[2]

A key strategy for reversing this conditioning is to bring to mind the previously painful experience while someone with you helps you keep from feeling the intense physiological response normally elicited by the experience. Each time this happens less and less of the negative emotion is felt and your experience becomes more detached. Here's an example. If you were bit by a dog as a child you might have a strong fear of dogs. You spend your whole life avoiding dogs or experiencing a great deal of stress whenever you encounter or think of encountering one. However, if after some time, you were exposed to dogs and they affectionately licked your hand, your fear of dogs might subside. In some cases, the fear might even go away. Because you were exposed to the item causing you emotional duress (the dog) but didn't have the painful experience immediately follow (being bit) your fear decreases as a result of these modified encounters. After a significant amount of time your fear may even go away. That's what psychologists call extinction.

Given the above example you can see why thinking about the hurtful event within a therapeutic setting might be helpful. By thinking about the hurtful experience with a therapist present the intensity of your physiological reaction can be adjusted and change your fearful angry response into one less intense. Just as

---

2. Everett J. Worthington Jr., "The Pyramid Model of Forgiveness," in *Dimensions of Forgiveness*, 119.

forcing yourself to smile can elevate your mood, thinking about a painful experience within a calm relaxed physiological state can lessen the negative impact that experience has on you. This strategy begins the extinction process. This first step is essential because it acknowledges you've been hurt but allows you to ease the emotional experience so you can transition to the next level of the process. In this next level, you're asked to develop a different understanding of the person who hurt you. If you can cause the sense of anger, fear, and anxiety brought about by being in the presence of the offending individual to subside you can begin to see him or her as less of a threat and more like another human being.

Level 2—Empathize with Those Who Hurt You

When Worthington talks about empathizing with the individual he's doing so to help you move past a fear based experience to one that's more detached from the individual. Worthington isn't saying you have to lay down and take what happened to you lightly, rather he's interested in finding ways for you to think differently about the perceived threat (The offending party and conditions surrounding the offense). In fact, what may appear as weakness is really a very strong response because it takes strength and courage to face what's happened to you particularly when it means facing pain again and again. If you can't think about the person who hurt you in a way that's anything other than threatening, you'll never escape from the cycle of fear, anger, or the "fight or flight" response that keeps you emotionally imprisoned. Fostering a specific type of empathy for your offender (and that's the key factor, it's a particular type of empathy) helps you move beyond the fight or flight experience to a more detached one. This transition frees you from the emotional turmoil brought about by thinking of and reexperiencing this individual and the situation in which they hurt you. Worthington says the following about this stage:

> We expect that a strong sense of compassionate empathy, which affects the above sources of feedback, will necessarily change the emotion and experience of

unforgiveness. The transformation is not necessarily full-blown forgiveness (at this point), but the experience of unforgiveness will have been modified.[3]

Worthington is basically using the physical, cognitive, and emotional connectivity discussed earlier to help weaken the negative emotional state one is experiencing and establish a means for viewing the offending party as another human being. This compassionate empathy allows us to discern the thoughts and feelings of another person, feel "with" the person, share similar emotional and mental states with the person, and ultimately have compassion and care for the person. Compassionate empathy is challenging but keeps us from viewing the offending individual as nothing more than a threatening object. Empathic compassion induces positive emotional associate feedback. This type of feedback helps you overcome your fear induced emotional experience trapping you in a negative emotional loop. When we experience the person who hurt us as another human being sharing a common human nature with us, the huge monster we believe that person to be dissipates and they become just another person. They're just as vulnerable to the failures and shortcomings of the human condition as we are. This new way of experiencing the individual transforms the negative emotional experience we've associated with them to be less threatening. This doesn't mean we're completely free from anger or frustration nor does it mean we aren't hurting, but the immediate threatening experience we had begins to disappear.

This level of engagement with the painful experience and the individual who hurt you isn't something you rush into. In fact, Worthington notes this stage takes time to process. By developing this empathic compassion, you view the offender as just another fallible human being. It doesn't excuse what they did nor negate your desire for justice, but you think about what happened in a more mindful way. You start to understand sometimes people hurt other people unintentionally, and even when done intentionally it's done because of their failures and shortcomings. The desired

---

3. Ibid., 120.

result of empathic compassion is to relocate your painful experience to a less emotionally powerful psychological space. While you still recognize how unjustly you've been treated, the level of negative emotional experience surrounding the event is reduced. You start to view the "threat" (That is the person who hurt you) as just another human being making bad choices, having bad things done to them, and for good or bad, struggling to fulfill the same needs every other human being has to fulfill such as love, support, care, and concern.

At this level, we're still not ready to forgive the person who hurt us. There's still a great deal of work to do in order for the act of forgiveness to occur. In fact, just because you can empathize with someone and understand why they treated you badly doesn't mean you forgive them. It simply means you're able to cognitively understand what may be the reasons for why this person treated you so badly. Forgiveness is still a choice you have to make and that comes in the next step.

Level 3—Giving an Altruistic Gift

At this level, Worthington recognizes simply having compassionate empathy isn't enough to experience forgiveness. Stopping at the previous level limits many of the benefits forgiveness offers. These previous two levels are important but they merely set the stage for the current level where the individual offers the altruistic gift of forgiveness. Remember, altruism is helping others, or at least extending good will to them without any regard for yourself. It's giving away a piece of who you are for the benefit of someone else. That requires making an intentional choice to do something. Worthington believes along with compassionate empathy we need a healthy sense of humility to be forgiving people. This seems counter intuitive given you're the person who got hurt. In no way is Worthington suggesting you're responsible for what happened to you and therefore must be humble enough to accept whatever abuse or negative treatment you've experienced. However, humility helps us recognize both the offender and sufferer are human beings and like those who hurt us, we are capable of hurting others as well. Perhaps we're not capable of a terrible crime or abuse but we're capable of hurting other people and probably have in one way or another. If we're capable of hurting other people and would like to be forgiven for doing so, perhaps we can extend the gift of forgiveness to someone who hurt us. Humility inclines our heart to see ourselves as we truly are. We are people capable of being hurtful toward others and in need of forgiveness just like anyone else.

The choice to give the gift of forgiveness is a major step forward and it's at this level the experience of forgiveness can give us our first taste of freedom. It still may not feel right; you still hurt, you've been treated unjustly, and part of you wants satisfaction for what was done, but by making this choice you've unlocked the key to reversing the psychological pain connected to the anger, frustration, and fear that has you trapped.

At this point it's hoped you can think about the hurtful experience with lower levels of negative emotional and psychological pain. You've started to have empathy for the person who hurt you, and are ready to be free from this negative experience. Now it's time to seriously commit to forgiving those who hurt you. You got here by recognizing everyone in this world hurts each other and you've been part of someone else's pain. You realize you're in need of forgiveness just like everyone else. Sure, you might not have perpetrated the same acts done to you, but you've hurt others and with this self-understanding you can be part of reversing the process of pain by extending forgiveness to someone else. This level allows you to make that choice.

Level 4—Commitment to Forgive

Committing to forgive someone requires you to eventually make public acts of forgiveness. These public acts are a catalyst for the reversal of the fear induced neurological paths still existing inside you. Public doesn't have to mean being in front of a large audience, it simply means taking this commitment to forgive residing in your mind and making it real by bringing it into the lived world which makes it much more real. The public nature of the act reduces the doubt lingering in your mind about whether or not you've truly forgiven your offender. Worthington explains this public act of forgiveness comes about gradually. It can start as a simple conversation between you and a trusted friend voicing you've forgiven the person who hurt you. You may want to create a "Certificate of Forgiveness" and keep it somewhere close by to reminded yourself you've forgiven the person who hurt you. This certificate might also be something you share with a therapist or friend as a tangible example that you've forgiven the offender. As a continued public expression of forgiveness, you might want to write a letter to the person who hurt you and read the letter out loud to your trusted friend, therapist, or pastoral minister. Then, if you find it necessary, send the letter or have a personal conversation with the person who hurt you. Of course, this last option would only be something you do if the situation permitted. Your safety and well-being must come first. What's important is through public acts of forgiveness the reversal of the negative psychological trauma caused by the offense continues to dissipate and the affirmation you need to believe you've forgiven the person who hurt you is reinforced. You should be able to recognize you've truly made the choice to forgive someone and you're acting on that choice in ways you're most comfortable. If you recall at the beginning of this chapter I discussed that we have control over our thoughts, feelings, and actions in varying degrees and each impacts the other in a holistic way. The area we have most control over is our actions. By making intentional public acts demonstrating we've forgiven someone we impact how we think about the person who hurt us. This public act (or continual public acts) becomes a catalyst for transforming our negative experiences into less intense emotional traps.

Level 5—Holding on to Forgiveness

Worthington believes people need to maintain some level of assurance they've forgiven their offender or else they begin to think they never forgave them in the first place. He believes explicit attention to maintaining forgiveness is important because the continued lingering of fear-conditioned neurologically mediated responses toward the offender are still present. Helping clients continually recognize they've forgiven the individual, teaching emotional management skills, and ultimately moving through the pyramid again and again can be a significant way to help them remain in a state of forgiveness. This final level may simply be a place to start walking through the levels of forgiveness again. This is important because forgiveness is first and foremost a choice but one you're convinced you've made only as the emotional and physical elements created by the trauma begin to dissipate. We may be able to intellectually understand we've forgiven someone but we only "feel" that way after a certain period of time has lapsed. Sometimes revisiting the different levels helps us recognize our feelings have become less and less intense therefore making the act of forgiveness feel more and more real.

Worthington's model is very good and has helped many people overcome strong negative emotional reactions to painful situations experienced at the hands of other people. His model started a great deal of psychological research in the area of forgiveness. The fact he roots his model in research connected to brain functions as well as the stimulus response mechanisms of our body gives his model strong credibility because it parallels what psychologists have known about our stress systems for some time. I like this model very much but for our purposes I want to share one more psychological model so we can identify a convergence of themes from psychology and theology at the end of this chapter. I'm not implying Worthington's model is incomplete, rather I think by sharing another well-respected model by another well respected psychologist you can see for yourself how much these two models share with the spiritual and theological practices of Christianity.

ENRIGHT'S MODEL OF FORGIVENESS: FOUR PHASES PROCESS MODEL

Robert Enright's process model of forgiveness isn't too different from Worthington's pyramid model. Both recognize forgiveness as essential for healing from past hurt and trauma. Both recognize empathy and the extension of goodwill as important factors in the forgiving process. Yet, unlike Worthington's model which is more like a set of layers one climbs Enright views forgiveness as a process in which someone moves through different phases. The fact there's so much overlap between these models is actually very good. When two researchers work independently and come up with almost identical results it means they've discovered essential elements of whatever it is they're studying. For our purposes the fact both men identify the same core elements of forgiveness gives us confidence that what we're learning is the essence of this Christian virtue.

Some Preliminary Thoughts

Enright's process values reflection. Before beginning the process of forgiveness Enright encourages his clients to think about the level of pain the hurtful incident has caused them. Enright values details in his process. He asks clients to identify each painful incident and assign a specific number to represent the level of pain they're feeling (i.e. 8 out of 10, etc.). Then the client is asked to recall what time of day the offense occurred, how he or she initially reacted to it, and even where the pain is physically felt in their body. Specific details are important because it helps clients assess the impact the emotional pain has on their lives. Quantifying the pain also allows the client to identify if they're feeling better about their situation or if they're actually becoming angrier about the incident that hurt them. Additionally, this detailed assessment helps clients discover whether or not they need more time to process their pain and the impact these wounds have on their lives. It's only after realizing the impact of being unforgiving that people find themselves in the position to decide whether or not forgiveness is the healing strategy they need to pursue. More time may be required to better understand what forgiveness really is because people often underestimate what's involved in the process. This preliminary stage helps clients define their emotional pain, identify how that pain is unfolding in their lives, and provides the therapist with a chance to educate clients on the nature of forgiveness.

I think it's important people reflect on how they've managed emotional pain in the past. In particular, its important they identify how they've stuffed emotional pain into other areas of their lives. This is essential for the healing process because one needs to know the nature of their injury before they can treat it. So many people relocate past emotional pain in their present relationships, feel it as bodily pain making themselves physically ill, or overinvest themselves in activities such as work, leisure, and exercise just to keep from processing what's hurting them. To use more psychological terms people often displace, repress, or project emotional pain to alleviate some of the emotional impact it has in their lives. Enright believes people need to really understand this pain if they're going to be healed. That's why this pre-phase is so important. It helps the client recognize how deeply he or she is hurt, acknowledge it, and then contemplate whether or not to move forward with the forgiveness process.

Phase I: Uncovering Your Anger

Once clients start taking initial steps to confront their pain, it's important they intentionally explore the impact that pain has had on their lives with more depth. This deeper exploration requires the client to think about whether or not they're ignoring anger, displacing it, or refusing to confront it in some other way. It's important to consider whether or not anger is manifesting itself in destructive ways in relation to one's physical health, relationships, or spiritual well-being. You need to ask yourself how the anger associated with being wronged is impacting your ability to find happiness and flourish as a human being. The key outcome of this phase is identifying how anger hasn't been a positive mechanism for dealing with your pain. Enright puts it this way:

> The Uncovering Phase is just that—an uncovering of your wounds . . . that you might have received as the other person was unfair to you . . . As you see your specific wounds, you will be in a better position to take steps to reduce or even eliminate many of them.[4]

This isn't the time to decide whether or not to forgive someone, it's merely a time for deeper exploration of what was initially identified in the earlier phase. It's a way to methodically explore your emotional wounds and their impact on your life. The decision to forgive is its own phase. What makes this phase different from the preliminary phase is it allows the individual to acknowledge and more precisely define the nature of their emotional wounds. It forces clients to look at their wounds more surgically to fully appreciate the impact they have on one's whole life. Think of it as a progression from what was done generally in the preliminary phase to a more concise objective exploration in this first phase.

Phase II: The Deciding Phase

In this phase, it's hoped the client has reviewed the extent and depth of not just their pain but the anger accompanying it. Once this triage of emotional pain is complete the client may be ready to decide on a course of action for addressing their psychological wounds in different ways. If the preliminary work was done well clients realize past efforts and strategies such as ignoring anger or expressing it negatively haven't helped. It doesn't mean the client chooses forgiveness as an alternative strategy yet, only that they recognize what's been done in the past hasn't worked. Of course, the desired outcome is to use forgiveness to resolve anger and pain, but this only comes after fully appreciating how previous strategies have failed. As Enright states:

---

4. Robert D. Enright, *The Forgiving Life*, 168.

The Christian Vocation of Forgiveness

> Some people consider this phase the most important and the most difficult because it is the crossroads of forgiveness. It is here that you take courage in hand and commit to the forgiveness path. You commit to change, and change of any kind, especially change as large as forgiveness, is a challenge.[5]

If the client chooses to move forward, then the deeper work of forgiveness can begin. If they choose not to that doesn't mean the process stops, rather it means the client spends more time exploring current and past strategies to resolve their hurt, anger, and pain. In Enright's process model, just like Worthington's pyramid model, there's movement back and forth. I think of this phase as a check point. The client is either ready to move forward or needs more time to work on exploring the pain and anger and to continue assessing the strategies they've been using in more detail. If the client is ready to continue they move to the next phase of the process.

Phase III: The Work Phase of Forgiveness

This phase overlaps Worthington's work the most. Enright identifies four main tasks in this phase. The first is understanding the offender. Enright asks you to consider how the pain and hurt in the offender's life might be related to the way they acted toward you. By attempting to understand the perpetrator it's hoped you'll foster an intellectual understanding of how people hurt other people because of broken relationships, pain, and psychological damage in their own lives. Recognizing people hurt other people because they themselves are hurt helps you understand you're not the problem. There's a greater web of events causing people to hurt one another. This makes sense when you recognize people are naturally relational and those relationships either foster positive or negative outcomes. There's a book written by Simon Baron-Cohen called *The Science of Evil* in which the author describes how the

---

5. Ibid., 176

brain develops pathways allowing us to empathize with other human beings based in part on how individuals are treated by others. Baron-Cohen notes in the book that severely abused children who become sociopaths tend to have maldeveloped neurological empathy pathways impairing their ability to show empathy toward others.[6] One might say living in a fallen world has caused sin to perpetuate itself even at the most basic biological level. Therefore, the more we know about the way the person who hurt us has experienced life, the more we can understand how past relationships, environmental factors, and the pain and suffering in his or her life may have led to the situation we find ourselves in now. That doesn't excuse how we've been treated, it's merely a way to intellectually make sense of our situation.

The second important task in this phase is the development of compassion for the person who hurt you. Developing compassion strengthens your understanding of the perpetrator as another human being. You recognize they're frail, weak, and susceptible to the same negative forces impacting the whole human condition. By developing compassion, you move from merely understanding why the person hurt you to experiencing the individual as a fellow broken human being. This isn't a way to make excuses for what's been done nor is it a way to become a masochist merely letting people walk all over you. It's a way to recognize the complexity of human behavior and the common human condition we all share which is susceptible to these complexities. When you have compassion for the person who hurt you, you begin to transition to the third task of this phase which is accepting the pain you're feeling and embracing the responsibility you have for stopping it from continuing in your life and the life of others (Particularly those most close to you). This is when healing begins. If we can accept what was done, get through it, and forgive, we have an opportunity to stop the anger dwelling in us from being directed toward other people. Enright says it like this:

---

6. Baron-Cohen, Simon. *The Science of Evil*

The Christian Vocation of Forgiveness

> It is important for you to consider bearing the pain of others' wounding you because you, as a wounded person who might not bear the pain, run the risk of wounding others. If you can stand up under the weight of the pain, under the weight of love withdrawing from you, you are giving a great gift to the world. If you think about it, you are taking the bold step of stopping this particular wound toward you from multiplying into many more wounds. You are stopping a cycle of wounding.[7]

By acknowledging we can be the person who stops this cycle from perpetuating itself on someone else our suffering begins to have meaning. Additionally, our suffering at the same time begins to subside. Anger subsides and eventually goes away by extending forgiveness and good will toward the person who hurt you. Like Worthington, Enright believes the extension of forgiveness must be public in nature, not merely a silent mental assent done in the privacy of our psychological world. It might start with a smile, a phone call, a visit, or a simple act of acknowledgement demonstrating you've forgiven this person for the specific hurt they caused you. Regardless of how you show it you need to act upon your decision to forgive. This is the fourth and final task of the work phase.

An important distinction in Enright's model is his recommendation to identify specific things that need forgiven and not just generally forgive someone overall. We may have to forgive someone for five specific things they've done to us. We have to work on each act of hurt using the tasks outlined above. For example, if your mother hurt you by what she said and in the way she treated you, it's important to work on each thing said as well as each hurtful act perpetrated on you. Just forgiving her generally doesn't work as effectively as being specific according to Enright. Each hurtful act needs processed. We can only gain a complete holistic sense of peace after processing each hurtful act. Enright believes we must explore "all" the pain associated with that individual, not just the general sense of pain we feel. As we forgive each

---

7. Robert D. Enright, *The Forgiving Life*, 187

act of hurt we become more and more free from the emotional trap our anger and resentment has created. When we've processed all these acts we become completely free and can grow in peace. He also argues this process takes a great amount of time, emotional investment, and courage. However, the result provides a sense of peace in the client's life and more importantly stops them from perpetuating pain and anger on other people.

Phase IV: The Discovery Phase

The purpose of this phase sounds a little misleading since a great deal of "discovery" has already been done. Enright describes the purpose of what happens in this phase in the following way:

> The central point of the discover phase of forgiveness is to learn about forgiveness, about yourself, about who you are as a person, about your purpose in life, and about other people. The Central point is to deepen your story of who you are, about how the world works, and about who others are.[8]

Some of this exploration was started in the previous phase. However, in this phase you begin to understand the meaning of your suffering and how forgiveness is part of a process freeing you from pain and stopping you from perpetuating that pain in your other relationships. If we just stopped in the third phase we might believe our suffering has no meaning and there is no purpose for which it can be used. However, if we really reflect on the meaning of our life, the greater purposes for which we exist, and how suffering is a part of that narrative, we can begin to see our life in a greater context. Enright believes this phase is important to help us come to terms with how suffering has impacted us. Enright encourages us to reflect on the fact we have experienced love and pain in our lives and both are part of our life narrative; our love story. He wants us to use the pain and suffering we choose to endure to become part of our narrative enabling us to live with love and purpose.

8. Ibid., 192

We don't accept pain just to be a martyr, we accept it so we can limit its effects on others and choose love instead. It doesn't mean ignoring our pain, it merely means once it has been processed it's not the predominant theme in our self-understanding. It means we accept some level of pain in order to live a greater narrative of love for others.

USING THEOLOGICAL AND PSYCHOLOGICAL INSIGHT TO BE A PERSON OF FORGIVENESS

Based on what we've discussed you can see there are many assumptions about people and the world that connect with Christian theological truths in both models of forgiveness. For example, the fact people were meant to experience love, be social, and connect with one another finds support in both psychology and Christian theology. As noted above, we're hurt by people when we feel they've withdrawn love from us and filled that void with painful acts, words, and intentions. Enright discusses the fact when people are hurt they have a tendency to perpetuate that hurt on others which is reflective of the way sin multiplies itself in a broken fallen world. In order to continue our discussion, I want to use the truths from psychology and theology to demonstrate how they converge upon one another. Then, in chapter 5, I will develop a practical approach to living the Christian vocation of forgiveness that can be applied daily and discuss some of the fruits this type of Christian living provides.

Preparing to Forgive

The world is full of hurt and pain. Some of you may have read the book, *The Giver* by Lois Lowry. The book speaks profoundly to the human desire to eliminate all forms of pain in life. In that book the world is recreated and people no longer feel strong emotions like passion or live within intimate human relationships. Everyone is friendly, kind, and seems content, but their emotional engagement with one another is very shallow. There's no real pain in this world, no hunger, disease, emotional turmoil, or difficult decisions to make. It's all taken care of through medication to dampen one's emotions, precise processes to eliminate the weak (regardless of age, newborn or elderly), and socially constructed regulations to maintain order and peace. It looks like utopia from the outside, but as the book demonstrates the life these people live is a shadow of real human living. Yet, because this society recognizes there is a need to remember the raw intensity of human life, they choose one person to keep the "memories" of the full range of human experience. He is the "Keeper of memories" and the one who is courageous and brave enough to know human joy, love, hope, and faith but also pain, suffering, destruction, and struggle. He is the one who bears the good and the bad of the human experience for the whole community. The point is for human life to be fully experienced we must suffer and feel pain along with joy, happiness, and pleasure. Suffering is the risk we take when we choose to love and live a full human life. In the book the gentleman teaching young Jonas to be the new "Keeper of memories" laments that in order for the community to live in the state of utopia they created they had to give up so much. They gave up the experience of color, sunshine, and the many dimensions of the human experience that makes living so profoundly deep. Color is given up so there is no discrimination, passion is taken away from people so there is no jealousy, and everything that makes life more than "satisfactorily livable" is done away with. Yet for them, the cost is worth never experiencing pain. The older gentleman training Jonas to be the new keeper of memories says:

> Sometimes I wish they'd ask for my wisdom more often-there are so many things I could tell them; things I wish they would change. But they don't want change. Life here is so orderly, so predictable-so painless. It's what they've chosen.[9]

---

9. Lois Lowry, *The Giver*, 103.

We can't choose a life without pain and I suspect we wouldn't want to if it means taking away our experience of love, pleasure, and other wonderful facets of living a human life. But because we want the richness of human living we must accept life involves getting hurt. In order to prepare ourselves to forgive people who hurt us we need to recognize hurt and pain occur intentionally and unintentionally. We are created to give and receive love but in a world broken and full of sin sometimes we fail to love others and other people fail to love us. We need to recognize we're trapped in our own experience and seldom rise above it to connect in some way to someone else's experience. We must accept the brokenness of life resulting from living in a broken sinful world.

In Enright's working and discovery phase he encourages clients to bear the pain inflicted on them to keep from perpetuating that pain on others. He sees the ability to absorb pain and defuse its effects as a gift, particularly a gift to the people you love. In his discovery phase Enright asks individuals to explore their life narrative. By looking honestly at one's life narrative someone can see they live a life in which they've been hurt but additionally have hurt others as well. Enright encourages us to discover the meaning and purpose of suffering and accept it as part of living in a broken world. Worthington's "Altruistic Gift" is the actual willingness to extend forgiveness to others because you're willing to humbly accept the fact you've probably hurt others as well. When we choose to love, we make ourselves vulnerable to being hurt and likewise, those who choose to love us sometimes get hurt because we didn't reciprocate that love. Both these theories recognize we live in a broken world and the love we were meant to share often gets taken from us. In order to prepare ourselves to be agents of forgiveness we need to recognize the world is not perfect, justice is not something we experience perfectly in this life, and only when Christ returns and completes what was started at the cross will people give and receive love perfectly. Until then, it's our role as the body of Christ to be agents and moments of grace. To be a forgiving person one must recognize they live in a broken world in which they get hurt, feel pain, and hurt others.

Making it Personal

If we accept we live in a broken world and get hurt by others; if we acknowledge sometimes, even when we don't mean it, we hurt other people, we need to reflect on our personal experience to identify how pain impacts our lives. When someone hurts us we can't just shake it off saying, "Oh well, that's just how life is." We need to acknowledge we're angry, depressed, sad, and feeling wounded. We need to think about how we're avoiding our feelings and in doing so over an extended period of time hurting ourselves physically, relationally, emotionally, cognitively, and spiritually. We need to take time to reflect on our pain and the many ways we're ignoring it. Then, we need to be honest with ourselves and acknowledge by not addressing our pain we're negatively impacting our lives in tremendous but subtle ways.

Christianity recognizes we're an enigma to ourselves. Part of living in a fallen world is no longer having an accurate sense of ourselves. If you recall at the beginning of this book I talked about how humanity's fall from grace impacts everything about who we are. It separates us from God, one another, and then from the rest of creation. In addition to sin's impact on all these areas, it separates us from ourselves. Ultimately that occurs when we die (i.e. the body is separated from the soul), but even in life, we struggle to understand who we are. It takes courage to look at ourselves and deal with the reality of our brokenness. Our natural inclination is to avoid this truth through a number of psychological coping mechanisms. We hide our hurt by taking it out on others. We avoid feeling our wounds by becoming obsessed with work, taking drugs, over eating, diving into pornography, and yes, even by becoming overly spiritual.

Our God is the God of truth. Hiding from the truth of our situation is in many ways hiding from God. We hide from God who is true holiness in order to keep from experiencing how far we are from being holy ourselves. In fact, if you remember, one of the first acts Adam and Eve did after disobeying God was to hide from him in the garden (Genesis 3:8–10). In the second phase of Enright's model we see him stressing the importance of acknowledging our hurt and recognizing how harboring that hurt has impacted how we feel, the relationships we have, and our worldview overall. We need to take the time to explore that hurt. No one likes to acknowledge being hurt. However, as Enright states, we often have to feel pain before we can heal. Just like going into the hospital for surgery and dealing with the pain of recovery, acknowledging and experiencing the pain caused by what someone has done to us is an important first step for healing. After we recognize we're living in a broken world we have to acknowledge how this brokenness has impacted us personally. We no longer run from our emotional pain, but embrace it, analyze it, acknowledge it, explore how it has negatively impacted us and others, and contemplate what to do with it.

Making the Choice

Forgiveness, like love, requires making a choice. Just because we accept the idea we live in a broken world, accept the fact we hurt others just as we've been hurt, and are feeling the pain of this perpetual condition of sin and brokenness, doesn't mean we're ready to forgive those who hurt us. Yet, in this stage we must make that choice if we're going to move forward. If we want to get past the mere self-analysis of why we're hurt and how it's impacting our life we need to make the decision to forgive those who hurt us. If we're not ready to do so that's okay, but we have to realize moving forward means deciding to forgive someone for what they've done. Worthington believes at some point in the process, preferably at the beginning, we need to accept we have been hurt, decide to heal, and avoid falling into the traps of cynicism and indifference. He believes you have to choose to overcome the temptation to be a victim and choose forgiveness over revenge. Enright notes this stage in the forgiveness process is when the individual stops relying on psychological defense mechanisms and chooses forgiveness. Ultimately, this is the time when the Christian decides to live out the true vocation they're called to exercise which is to be a living icon of Christ's forgiveness in a broken world.

We're all created to be image bearers of the living God. We reflect that image in a number of ways. While we're all expected to be people who love God first, one another, and care for creation, the actual manner in which this is carried out is filtered through our personal and individual situations. Forgiveness likewise manifests itself in our lives in a unique way. It requires the Christian to take up the cross and accept the responsibility they have to forgive others. There's some level of personal cost to being a forgiving individual. The revenge and justice we naturally desire must be tempered by the virtue of forgiveness. Forgiving someone isn't a feeling we experience at first, it's a choice we make just as love is first and foremost a choice. Our task is to decide to be the very thing our Christian vocation asks of us which is to be an active agent of forgiveness in a broken world. We come to a place where we accept the conditions of living in a sinful world and decide to follow a Christian way of life that includes acts of forgiveness and love.

SUMMARY OF CHAPTER 4

Throughout this chapter, we've explored two seminal works regarding forgiveness from a psychological perspective and identified how these theories connect with Christian theological principles. These can help us understand the basic foundational principles where psychology and Christian theology connect, but the next question becomes what can I do on a regular basis to integrate these ideas into my life? How can I become that active agent of love and grace in the world I occupy discussed in this chapter? These are the questions I hope to answer for you in the next chapter.

5

Exercising Forgiveness and the Fruits of a Forgiving Life

HABIT IS OUR BEST friends. Depending on what we habitually do, we can become masters of virtue or masters of vice. It's the very thing that makes us experts in our professions and at the same time sets us on a lifetime path of poor eating, a sedentary lifestyle, and cigarette smoking. Aristotle once wrote, "Excellence is an art won by training and habituation. We do not act rightly because we have virtue or excellence, but we rather have those because we have acted rightly. We are what we repeatedly do. Excellence, then, is not an act but a habit."

I believe we can become agents of grace if we regularly practice the virtue of forgiveness. In this chapter, I'll do two things. First, I'm going to map out the general ideas necessary to begin a daily practice of forgiveness. If you choose to make this process part of your daily spiritual practices I believe you can become a truly forgiving human being. The work is hard, emotionally draining, but very fulfilling. Secondly, I want to demonstrate how forgiveness is beneficial to everyday living and human flourishing. Research shows there are numerous physical, emotional, and relational benefits to being a forgiving person. While Christians by their very vocation are called to be agents of forgiveness, the very fact human beings were meant to function a particular way, a forgiving and relational way, means when we do so we live better lives. How can you practice forgiveness? Let's look at that right now.

DOING THE FORGIVING—ALLOWING THE HOLY SPIRIT TO CLARIFY YOUR PAIN

If you spent time reviewing the above theories of forgiveness and pondering the theological points I presented earlier, you may be ready to work through your own pain and embrace forgiveness. I'm going to provide you with daily practical steps to facilitate forgiveness in your life and free you from the anger, guilt, and fear keeping you from loving and being loved as God intended. Drawing on the spiritual elements of Christianity and the psychological processes outlined in the previous chapter, you can take concrete steps to be a more forgiving person. Here's what a day framed in forgiveness looks like.

First, quiet yourself and find a place where you won't be disturbed. Ask the Holy Spirit to dwell with you and enlighten your heart showing you the emotional scars and wounds created by the pain you've been experiencing. Ask the Spirit to comfort you and pour God's grace upon you. Pray at least a good five minutes making yourself aware of the Holy Spirit's presence in the healing process.

Next, remind yourself you live in an imperfect world. That means not only have you been hurt by other people, but you've most likely hurt others as well. Dwell with this fact; life isn't fair, all we have that's good is a gift from a loving God. There's nothing good without him and be thankful for God's goodness. However, remember how deep sin runs in the world. Think about how sin is nothing more than disordered love and when we don't love properly we hurt one another. Much of the pain you feel is because love has been disordered in your life. Since you were created to give and receive love the pain you feel comes from the fact you can't love others as you were intended and you don't receive love as you need. This lack of and inability to love is the result of others experiencing the same imperfect love you've experienced. Remember this broken world has developed into a system that by default leads to pain and suffering. Yet also remember with Christ there's healing and love. Decide to avoid being cynical and perpetually wounded by this emotional pain and be healed. You can choose not to be a victim of your circumstances and avoid the trap of perpetuating pain and suffering. Remember, you can be an agent of grace. If we just allow God to carry out the required justice in the world we free ourselves of that burden to be agents of his mercy, grace, and love. You can choose to stop the cycle of pain and become a living icon of God's healing grace. Take the time to commit to these ideas and then consider moving to the next step of forgiveness. If you're not ready, that's okay. Just dwell here for as long as you need and come back to this place of contemplation as often as you need.

With the enlightenment of the Holy Spirit acting in your life and the acceptance of the fact the world is fallen and broken, explore your heart for anger, guilt, and pain. Someone has hurt you. They've treated you unjustly and kept you from experiencing the love you need to thrive. They made you nothing more than an object for their own ends. You've been abused, criticized, improperly treated, ignored, pushed aside, and betrayed. In a fallen world people treat one another this way, sometimes without even knowing it. Where in your heart are you harboring feelings of anger and pain? Where have you pushed them deep down inside refusing to acknowledge them? How have they caused you shame and guilt? Are your relationships with other people, with God, and with yourself negatively impacted because you carry this anger around? Ask the Holy Spirit to help you become aware of the effect this anger, guilt, and pain has on your life and how it has perpetuated itself in others. Again, dwell here as long as you are comfortable before moving on.

At this point step back from the reflection on your pain. Only do as much of this as you're willing to bear. However, be brave. Come back to this point again another time, whether it's in the same day or the next. The point is to keep working this process every day and move through it as God leads you. The more you allow the Spirit to enlighten you regarding your pain and anger and its impact on the rest of your life the closer you come to moving forward in the forgiving process. As you continue your reflections become more and more specific about 1) who it was that hurt you, 2) the specific incident that occurred, 3) the level of pain the event caused you, and finally 4) how it has negatively impacted your life. Start a list and keep a journal of who it was that hurt you and the specific things they did that causes you pain. Keep the journal with you and make part of your prayer moments throughout the day a time to reflect on these incidents and ask the Holy Spirit to help you feel compassion for those who hurt you. Do this again and again, day after day, until you're ready to actually forgive the person for what they've done.

DOING THE FORGIVING—RELEASING THE ANGER

You can spend a great deal of time exploring your pain and considering whether or not to extend forgiveness to the people who hurt you. It's not an easy decision and it takes courage to do so. If you've come this far, you've begun to experience your pain and suffering by thinking about who hurt you, how they did so, and the level of the pain each incident has caused you, but up to this point you've stopped going any further. If you're comfortable doing so, it's time to move forward and forgive the person for what they've done. If you're ready to forgive them, here's what you need to do next.

First, in the presence of God, bring yourself back to the place and conditions surrounding your pain. Remember the experience and feel the emotions that come with it. "Remembering" is a powerful spiritual tool. We often think of remembering as a purely psychological experience, but it has great spiritual significance as well. For example, God asked the Israelites to "Remember" the Passover every year. Remembering the Passover isn't a distant experience for the Israelites to simply talk about, they literally relive the Passover experience. This is what the word "Remember" actually describes; a "re-membering", putting back together of an experience from the past to be a present reality in the moment. This is an important element in the Jewish celebration of Passover. The

The Christian Vocation of Forgiveness

Mishnah Pesachim, a set of writings by Jewish Rabbis is a redaction of the oral tradition of the Torah. It was written in the third century and captures the heart of Jewish beliefs as understood by the Rabbis of the time. It carries a great deal of weight and is held in high regard when it comes to understanding Jewish Law. In it we read the following about the Passover ritual:

> Rabban Gamliel used to say, "Anyone who has not mentioned these three things on Pesach has not discharged his obligation, and these are [the items that he must mention]: the Pesach sacrifice, matsa and bitter herbs. [The] Pesach [Passover] sacrifice [is offered]—because the Omnipresent passed over the homes of our ancestors in Egypt. Matsa [is eaten]—because our ancestors were redeemed in Egypt. Bitter herbs [are eaten]—because the Egyptians embittered the lives of our ancestors in Egypt." ***In every generation a person must see himself as though he [personally] had gone out of Egypt***, as it is stated, "And you shall tell your son on that day, saying, 'It is because of what the Lord did for me when I came forth out of Egypt'" (Exodus 13:8). Therefore we are obligated to thank, praise, laud, glorify, exalt, lavish, bless, extol, and adore He Who made all these miracles for our ancestors and for us: He brought us out from slavery to freedom, from sorrow to joy, from mourning to [celebration of] a festival, from darkness to great light, and from servitude to redemption. [Therefore,] let us say before Him, Halleluyah!—Pesachim 10:5

Remembering is a powerful spiritual tool we can use to forgive events from the past. We use it to reexperience the hurt we feel in order to address that pain and allow it to dissipate from our bodies. You may recall in Worthington's model of forgiveness he requires clients to recall the memory of being hurt and the pain that comes with that memory in order to experience the negative emotions in a non-threatening way. Doing so leads to the deprogramming of the body's stress system. After doing this a number of times a reduced experience of pain, anger, and shame emerge in parallel to the body's reduced fight or flight response. Once this reduction occurs, you are able to process the negative experience in a more mindful way.

The first step of forgiving someone is to allow yourself to make present the past hurtful experience along with the pain and anger you're feeling. This gets the negative emotions out into the open instead of hiding them inside and letting them impact your life. Just as recovery from surgery and other medical interventions makes your body sore causing you pain while healing, recovery from emotional wounds involves pain during the healing process as well. Share that pain with God; he is strong, understanding, and can help you carry the burden. Experience the pain so you can recover from it, don't ignore it and allow it to fester inside like an infected cyst.

Secondly, with that painful experience pray that the Holy Spirit helps you find meaning in your suffering. Yes, you suffer because of a fallen sinful world as explained above, but your suffering isn't in vain. There's redemption found within it and meaning and purpose can be derived from it. Christians must exercise the virtue of hope even in the midst of pain and suffering. In order to do so, we need to find meaning within the context of our suffering. Most likely you've already created negative meaning around the experience. Perhaps you believe you suffer because "All people are evil" or "You deserve to suffer." These types of "meaning" are tainted by despair. Redemptive remembering, the kind of remembering God asks us to exercise finds hope and a higher purpose in the suffering. When Christ gave us the Eucharist he asked us to perform that simple meal as an act of redemptive remembering; a type of making present his death and suffering but also his resurrection. When we remember while attempting to make meaning of our suffering we do so in order to see the resurrection in it. We accept the fact we're no longer victims of these experiences but survivors. Redemptive remembering shows us a new life by introducing us to a life of hope and grace birthed from the old life of pain, anger, suffering, and guilt.

In addition to making meaning of our suffering we need to recall in our redemptive narrative that we've hurt other people and those people have forgiven us of our transgressions. We need to remember what it feels like to be forgiven and the peace that comes with it. When we recall what it felt like to be forgiven we know first-hand the gift we are extending to the one who hurt us. This is grace in action. Not that we naturally want to extend this gift, but that we can transcend ourselves and allow God to work through us. We are agents of grace; it's our purpose and gives our lives meanings. We follow a God who is love and as creatures created in his image we flourish best when we reflect that goodness. Because we know there is grace and life for those who embrace the Christian way, we find redemption even in our suffering. We grow from our suffering, we become stronger, and we explore the depths of the human experience because we allow ourselves to be vulnerable to the good and bad experiences of love. God understands your suffering and will walk with you through it. The Christian God is a God who doesn't totally transcend suffering because he embraced suffering as the God/man Jesus Christ. Retell your story from a redemptive point of view. Do so with a proper understanding of who God is. If you believe God desires you to suffer, you have a poor image of our loving God. If you need a refresher on what God is like, go back to chapter two and reread the material on "The God Image."

The best way to demonstrate for you what a redemptive narrative looks like is to share one with you. Here is an example of what a redemptive narrative looks like based on the experience a client of mine had. You'll find in it the need to find meaning and purpose in her suffering and the ability to see how God can make right what has been made wrong.

I was working with a young woman in the process of getting a divorce. Her husband was a well-respected Pastor. She was given limited visitation with her son who lived with her ex-husband in the family home. She had to leave the home because it was owned by the church and was forced to live in an apartment in another section of town. My client believed life had meaning and purpose only when it followed her previous narrative. In that narrative, she married a Godly man, had children, and lived as a Pastor's wife.

If the narrative veered from that storyline in any way life lost its meaning and purpose. Divorce, particularly a messy divorce and separation from her child was not part of the narrative. When she found herself in such a situation she despaired, was hurt, and believed life had lost all sense of meaning and purpose. She was no longer the person she believed she was meant to be. She was angry and harbored negative feelings for her husband for years. She no longer had control over her narrative and it was unfolding in ways that caused her terrible grief. She was in distress because the narrative she expected to live was in conflict with the narrative she was experiencing. Understandably this caused her a great deal of pain and confusion. Who she was and what she became made her angry. She felt nothing but hatred toward her ex-husband.

My client had difficulty interpreting the meaning of her narrative. She felt no redemption in her suffering. This conflict caused her deep psychological distress not just because of her separation and subsequent loneliness, but also because the way she believed her life was going to unfold didn't unfold that way at all.

In order to facilitate a more redemptive understanding of her story I asked her questions about how her issues with her husband started, what her situation might mean, etc. I was helping her rewrite her story in a way that gave her situation meaning and purpose. She filled in the gaps, I was just a co-author. My function was to challenge her and reframe events in her life so she could take control of the story and rewrite it in a way that demonstrated there was meaning and purpose in her suffering. She needed to understand suffering could become a means of transformation that is positive and life giving. She started to explore what it meant to be a Christian woman who loves her child yet finds herself in a position separated from him and working outside the home. I asked her if there were any other Christian women in similar situations and what their lives say about her story. I helped her identify strong women who stepped outside expected roles from the bible and asked her to reflect on them and identify if her story connected to them in any way. As we explored these options she began to discover a connection in her story to these other narratives and developed a ministry for divorced Christians in her new church. As her story about suffering became more redemptive she was able to forgive her ex-husband and move forward with her life. She became free of the anger and pain that emerged each time she thought of her former life and embraced forgiveness as a means to take the narrative further. Life did not stop with divorce, it emerged from the pain brought about in the context of that situation and found new meaning.

I read a great book called *The Road We Must Travel, A Personal Guide for Your Journey* that contained a number of chapters by Christian authors giving advice on spiritual topics. In one of those chapters about suffering Tullian Tchividjian writes the following:

> Instead of looking to Jesus for our significance and value, we look to insignificant things. When that happens, we become slaves. God comes after us in the person of Jesus Christ, not angrily to strip away our freedom, but affectionately to strip away our slavery to self so that we might become truly free . . . The reason for our anger and bitterness in the crucible of suffering is that God is prying open our hands to take away something we've held onto more tightly than we've held onto him.[1]

To be a forgiving person we need to find redemption in our pain and let go of whatever is keeping us from the freedom we have in Christ. Maybe my client was holding on to the image of being a stay at home mom and Pastor's wife more than she was holding on to being one who walks with the risen Lord.

The last thing we need to do in this process of forgiveness is to perform some action that concretely demonstrates we've forgiven the person who hurt us. This can be as elaborate as a formal letter written and mailed to the person or as simple as merely stating you've forgiven that person out loud to trusted friends. The key is doing something concrete and not just keeping the idea of forgiveness in your head. Forgiveness is not just a psychological process, it's a spiritual process as well. Human beings need concrete expressions of inner spiritual experiences. Why do we baptize with water,

---

1. Tullian Tchividjian, "Trouble Happens," in *The Road We Must Travel*

use bread and wine at the Lord's supper, and anoint with oil? It's not because these things in and of themselves have magic, it's because they give concrete expression to inner spiritual experiences. The exercise of forgiveness needs the same concrete expression to sink in. We need to find tangible ways to demonstrate forgiveness and be able to repeat them again and again. We need to concretely express our forgiveness and not just express it in our minds. The more we're able to make our choice to forgive someone feel concrete, the more likely we'll experience the sense that we've truly forgiven them.

I was working with a couple in therapy who were overcoming infidelity. The husband became so detached from his wife that she found comfort in another man's company. This relationship grew to where she cheated on her husband. The two worked hard to reconcile but were struggling to forgive one another. He was struggling to forgive her for her infidelity and she was struggling to forgive him for leaving her emotionally starved. We worked the forgiveness process together and they made great progress. As a final act of forgiveness, they wrote down the things they forgave one another for and built a fire in their backyard. Then, taking what they wrote down in their hands walked over to the fire and burned the lists together as a sign that all was indeed forgiven. This act gave them a deeper sense that what was done in the past was done. It's these types of rituals that help take cognitive decisions and make them concrete experiences so the feeling of forgiveness can take root.

This is how you do the work of forgiveness. It's a two-part process. The first is to spend time in the presence of God reflecting on how you were hurt by someone and keep yourself from hiding and running from that hurt. The second is to go through the above steps of re-experiencing the pain you suffered in the presence of God. When you do that, you're giving that experience a new redemptive meaning and purpose. Then, when you come to that place you're ready to extend the gift of forgiveness in a tangible way you do it. You forgive and express that forgiveness in whatever way is comfortable for you to do so. All of this helps you see the offender as just another person suffering from a lack of love and unable to love others as intended by God.

A CONCISE PATH TO THE PRACTICE OF FORGIVENESS

We can synthesize the work of Worthington, Enright, and the theological ideas presented earlier into seven basic steps. It's important to remember these steps should be done prayerfully inviting the Holy Spirit into the process in two distinct ways. First, ask the Holy Spirit to be with you when your emotions become too powerful to bear alone. This process can bring up some powerful feelings and you'll often need supernatural strength to continue healing and exploring your wounds. Secondly, ask the Spirit of God to clearly reveal the different facets of pain you're experiencing. Sometimes we can't see our wounds because we've covered them up with so many layers of dysfunction they're no longer visible. You need the Holy Spirit to open your eyes to your pain so you can recover from it. Here's the seven step process I use for myself and when working with clients that concisely employs everything we've talked about in this book so far:

Step 1: Committing to a Christian Worldview

Remember the world is a fallen and broken place. Injustice and disordered love are part of that brokenness and the main reasons we hurt one another. People were created by a God who is love. Because God is love and we were created to reflect that love, we're meant to give and receive love. When we don't do that, we suffer.

Forgiveness is a way to break the pattern of hurt, pain, and anger caused by our broken life. By offering forgiveness we free ourselves from being spiritually trapped in hate, revenge, anger, and self-destructive habits.

An important note for this step is to root your Christian worldview in a healthy understanding of who God is, who people are, and why we do the hurtful things we do. These worldview elements are explained in Chapters 1 and 2 so if you believe God intends you to suffer or that people and creation are not intended to be good, revisit those chapters and spend time developing a healthy and accurate Christian worldview to foster the foundation necessary to be forgiving.

Step 2: Understanding Why You Were Hurt

This part of the process takes the general ideas from a Christian worldview and helps you view them on a more personal level for your given situation. The hope is you start to have at least some understanding of why the person who hurt you did what they did. Who is it that hurt you? What's your relationship to them? What did they do to you? How badly are you hurt by their actions, words, and behaviors? Given what you know about human nature, why might this person have hurt you? Has love been taken from them? Are they perpetuating the pain in their lives on you? Has their past been part of why they did what they did?

This phase of forgiveness helps you take a very emotional experience and step away from it so you can gain some psychological distance from the pain. By trying to understand why this individual hurt you a more mindful understanding of the experience can emerge and you can look at it more clearly and less emotionally. You may have to spend a great deal of time in this phase in order to move to the third step which involves assessing how effective you've been in dealing with your pain. Take whatever time you need, each step should be processed before moving to the next.

Step 3: Assessing Alternative to Forgiveness

You've tried a number of ways to deal with the pain, guilt, and anger associated with being wounded by another human being. You've stuffed it down into your soul, you've expressed it by perpetuating its effects on other people in your life, or you've carried out revenge only to find what you believed would be satisfying made you feel even worse. You need to really assess how well your current strategies have failed you. To do that, ponder the following points:

- How have you avoided the pain caused by the incident?
- How have you let your wounds stop you from doing things?
- How has the pain impacted you physically, mentally, emotionally, in your relationships, and in your spiritual life? What has been the personal fallout you've experienced by not exercising forgiveness and using these alternative strategies to deal with your pain?
- How have your wounds kept you from loving others and being loved?
- How much has being hurt impacted the way you understand the world? How has it skewed your worldview?

Like before, spend as much time as you need in this phase before moving forward. It's okay if it takes longer than anticipated, you need to be comfortable assessing how what you've been doing is ineffective. The key outcome of this phase is to recognize the strategy you're using isn't working and the only true path to emotional healing is forgiveness.

Step 4: Developing Empathy and Compassion

While the above stages utilize your cognitive resources allowing you to rationally understand why you've been a victim of someone's cruelty and assess how well you've managed the resulting emotional pain, this stage attempts to address your emotional experience. The hope is you'll develop some sense of empathy and compassion for the person who hurt you without going so far as to make you believe you "deserve" to be hurt. Having empathy for the person who hurt you is not the same as justifying what was done to you.

Ask the Holy Spirit to convict you once again about the truths regarding this broken and fallen world. People suffer because the system that drives a broken world is one of sin and pain. You've been hurt by someone who is also a hurting broken human being.

Try and recognize one reason this person treated you the way they did is because they're not dealing with emotional pain in a healthy way. Think about how hurt they must be for them to hurt you the way they did. See the world through their eyes. Try and appreciate they're the way they are because of how they've been treated. Try and appreciate how their upbringing and experiences of hurt, anger, and guilt have twisted their ability to give and receive love.

Remember there have been times when you either intentionally or unintentionally hurt other people. If you've been forgiven by these people remember how good it felt when they told you they forgave you. If you never heard words of forgiveness for something you've done, remember how that felt. We all hurt one another and at some point, need forgiveness.

It's important we develop a sense of empathy for the person who hurt us for one main reason. Empathy allows us to view them as another human being. Often, we think of them as a scary horrific monster because of how much pain they've produced in our lives. They may be a very bad person however, they're still just another human being suffering from the impact of a sinful and broken world just like you and me. It doesn't justify what they've done but it allows you to see them for what they are; just another scared struggling human being trying to love and be loved albeit in a twisted and broken way. Spend as much time as you like in this phase and don't feel you have to move forward until you're ready. In fact, if you have to go back to the other phases feel free to do so. You have to process these first four phases before moving on. The next step in the process is extending forgiveness to the individual who hurt you. Before you can do that, you need to have a clear understanding of why the world is the way it is (World View), why the individual who hurt you probably acted the way they did (Intellectual Understanding), and some level of emotional understanding of why they did what they did (Empathy/Compassion). You also recognize what you've been doing to deal with your emotional pain up to this point hasn't worked. While all this insight is good, what's next? If everything you've tried up to this point hasn't freed you from the effects of the wound, what can you do to heal? What's left? Forgiveness.

Step 5: Extending Forgiveness

Most of us like to give gifts. Forgiveness is just that, it's a gift. The problem is we usually don't like to give gifts to people who have treated us badly. At Christmas, most of us don't go looking for people who cheated us, stole from us, physically abused us, emotionally tortured us, or acted in some other awful way and say, "Hey, here's something I'm giving you that you don't deserve." Yet for forgiveness to work that's exactly what you have to do. Here is what you need to do in this step of the process:

- Pray to the Holy Spirit asking God to give you courage to walk through this shadow of death and embrace the path of forgiveness.

- Up to this point you know people hurt one another because of sin and disordered love in the world (Worldview), You've come up with logical reasons why this individual wounded you even though those reasons are completely distorted (Understanding), you can appreciate that the removal of love in this person's life and their inability to love has impacted them (Empathy/Compassion), and finally that your way of dealing with this emotional mess just hasn't worked (Decision Time). Think about these again to make sure you're ready for the decision to forgive. If not, it's okay revisit the previous steps, but if so, move forward.

- Decide to forgive. Let go of your need for justice, revenge, and restitution; it's gone. It's not an option any more so just let it go. This is the gift you offer the person who hurt you, a complete denouncement of what is rightfully yours so they no longer have any connection to you. The debt they owe you is removed. Your decision to forgive them means they no longer have psychological space in your head. Let it go and believe you've let it go.

- Publicly express this forgiveness in any of a number of ways. First, tell someone close to you that you've forgiven a person for what they've done. Tell as many people as appropriate but let it be public that you have forgiven _____ for the fact they did _____ to you. If you need to do more write a letter to that individual but don't send it. If you're comfortable at some point doing so, send it. If it's safe to do so, tell the person who hurt you they are forgiven in person. Whatever you need to do, do it, but do so publicly.

- Pray a prayer of forgiveness for that person out loud. Use the voice God gave you to speak into existence the choice of forgiveness you've made. You need to make real what is merely in your head and you do that through public behaviors, even behaviors as simple as telling another person what you've decided to do. It makes things real.

By making the decision to forgive the person who hurt you and making it public you've made something in your mind a reality. You're acting on your decision with each public act and vocal prayer. But even when you make the decision to forgive someone you still feel hurt. What can you do with this pain? In the past, knowingly or unknowingly you were able to avoid it by stuffing it down inside and hurting yourself or others. You either drank it away, avoided relationships with others, acted out in a hurtful way to those close to you, or simply closed yourself off from the world. You did something with it, but most likely, what you did was not helpful. What do you do with it now? You just allowed yourself to accept a great injustice. What do you do with all the pain that acceptance has caused? This is the Christ moment. This is when you do exactly what Christ did and accept the pain and redeem the experience through redemptive remembering and creating a redemptive narrative. That's the next step.

Step 6: Creating Your Redemptive Narrative

In order to have that pain dissipate, it has to have meaning and purpose and fit into your life narrative. Our pain is part of what has brought us to this point and can be a powerful motivator for living differently and moving forward. You can create a new redemptive narrative in the following way:

- Pray again that the Holy Spirit enlightens you to see your acceptance of suffering in light of a greater purpose. At the minimum, your acceptance of suffering reflects the acceptance of Christ's suffering. He suffered but not in vain and likewise your suffering is not in vain. It can be transformed into an expression of love simply because you choose not to let it impact other people. You're a member of the body of Christ so while suffering impacts the body, the body is also able to redeem that suffering because you're in Christ and Christ is in you. No one is asking you to be a doormat or a masochist, but rather to be strong and Christlike.

- In order to identify how suffering can lead to greater meaning and purpose, reflect on the story of Joseph. If you recall, Joseph had been betrayed by his brothers, sold into slavery, imprisoned, and treated as nothing more than an animal. Part of his life was a life of suffering. Yet, God used his suffering and Joseph was able to find favor in Pharaoh's eyes because of his ability to take bad situations and make them better. Joseph is put in charge of the whole country of Egypt during a famine and all the other countries in that region come to him to buy grain. Joseph's brothers must do the same so when they come to Joseph and find out he has become a powerful man who could kill them all for what they've done, they fear for their lives. Joseph however, embraces them as his own and says the following, "Even though you intended to do harm to me, God intended it for good, in order to preserve a numerous people, as he is doing today." (Genesis 50:20) Your story is a Joseph story; all Christian suffering finds its meaning in how it can be transformative making what seems like darkness light. It is the resurrection narrative actualized in our own life.

- Remind yourself the pain you feel can become a redemptive act and when you forgive someone you begin the process of eliminating that pain in your life and embracing a new sense of who you are and what God intends to do with you.
- In the end, by creating a redemptive narrative you're empowered to love yourself, others, and the good God who created you. This is the end purpose of forgiveness.

The above reminders and reflections help you develop a redemptive narrative. Now, how do you live out that narrative? How do you make sure the forgiveness you offer is a permanent part of your life experience? That's accomplished in step seven.

Step 7: Living Your Redemptive Narrative

This last step may seem redundant but it's one of the most important you will take to truly actualize the forgiveness you've extended to someone. Because emotions take time to change, we have to be certain we "believe" we've forgiven someone and begin to live and act as if it were true (Because it is) so that over time we begin to feel as if that person is forgiven. The narrative we've developed is important in this step. We have to share our narrative with others. The more we share the narrative the more we know it's true and not merely a fantasy. One great way of sharing your redemptive narrative is through a journal. Write about your experience of living life with the wounds you carry and then what life is like now that you've decided to forgive the person who hurt you and be healed. Join a support group or just be a part of a community in which you can contribute and use your story to help others. Whatever it takes, share your narrative. Here are the key elements you want to tell yourself and others as you begin to live into your redemptive narrative. These are also great elements to use if you do decide to journal:

- How does your narrative start, what brought you to the place of being wounded?
- How did the lack of love in your life make you vulnerable to being wounded?
- How did being wounded impact your ability to love others?
- How did being wounded impact your physical, mental, emotional, social, and spiritual well-being?
- How has healing started to change the way you think and behave?
- How did the pain you felt become a motivating force for the positive changes you're making now?
- What does your wound look like after some time of living a life of forgiveness? Has it healed? Are there scars? Can you look at the scar as a badge of courage; a reminder that you're a survivor and a strong courageous person?

These are important parts of your narrative and worthy of being shared with others. While it sounds overly simplistic, the best thing you can do after forgiving someone is "Fake it till you make it." These steps can free you from your emotional pain, you just need to follow the process. Take the time to work through it, believe you've forgiven those who hurt you, and act upon these beliefs. Forgiveness is a choice, you just need to restructure your life to live out what that choice means and as time goes by you'll feel the freedom you've elected to experience.

These seven steps are a convergence of all the theological and psychological ideas I've presented so far in this book. If you take the time and walk through them you can be healed. I challenge you to make the time to work on them. While there's never a guarantee the pain will completely go away, these steps can reduce the impact they've had on your life and certainly open your heart to give and receive the love that might just have been lacking before.

THE BENEFITS OF FORGIVENESS

We've talked a great deal of why forgiveness is important and how one exercises forgiveness, but now we need to discuss the benefits of being a forgiving person so we can appreciate why going through so much pain can be good for us. As a psychology professor, I often find myself needing to remind my students we're not merely brains locked in a biological container driven by physiological needs. Because I work at a Christian university I also find myself needing to remind them we're not merely spirits trapped in a body as well. In the first chapter of this book I demonstrated human beings are holistic creatures consisting of bodies, minds, emotions, relationships, and spirits. All these facets of our being are intertwined so tightly that when something impacts one area it impacts all the others as well. You cannot abuse your body without impacting your relationships, how you think, what you feel, and your spiritual life. Every behavior or action in any of these spheres impacts the others. These spheres of human living are not isolated from one another.

Because of this holistic existence it's important to recognize forgiveness impacts all areas of human life. When I forgive someone I'm not merely healing emotional wounds I'm also healing my body, spirit, mind, and relationships. All of who I am is impacted by what appears to be this simple cognitive choice to forgive others. In the 1662 book of common prayer there's a uniquely worded prayer of general confession. Unlike what you find in more contemporary Anglican prayer books, the 1662 version's use of English tends to make this point about our interrelated spheres of living impacting one another. In the wording below this holistic sense of how sin impacts us holistically is captured beautifully. The prayer reads as follows:

> Almighty, and most mercifull Father, We have erred and strayed from thy wayes like lost sheep, We have followed too much the devices, and desires of our own hearts, We have offended against thy holy laws, We have left undon those things which we ought to have don, And we have don those things which we ought not to have

The Christian Vocation of Forgiveness

don, ***And there is no health in us***, But thou, O Lord, have mercy upon us miserable offenders; Spare thou them, O God, which confess their faults, Restore thou them that are penitent, According to thy promises declared unto mankind in Christ Jesus our Lord; And grant, O most mercifull Father, for his sake, That we may hereafter live a godly, righteous, and sober life, To the glory of thy holy Name. Amen. (Emphasis added) [2]

Note the verse I've made obvious through italicized and bold text! This rendition of the general confession recognizes that sin, a spiritual ailment, impacts us to the point in which we profess to have "No health in us." This conclusion in the prayer envisions human beings as holistic creatures in which spiritual illness is as harmful as physical disease. Likewise, this observation implies being healed of our sin leads to a holistic experience of healing. Forgiveness is a healing act with positive effects for our whole being.

From a mental health perspective, there's a great deal of evidence demonstrating forgiveness has a positive effect on emotional trauma. Enright notes in his book, *The Forgiving Life* that after numerous studies the people he and his team worked with improved significantly in their emotional health. Decreases in anxiety and depression as well as improvements in self-esteem are all the result of a number of scientific experiments Enright and his team completed over the course of numerous research studies.[3] This research parallels other studies demonstrating a great deal of benefits to one's overall well-being because they've grown to be more forgiving people. Lordes Rey and Natalio Extremera published an article in the *Journal of Health Psychology*[4] demonstrating forgiveness is positively correlated with a health-related quality of life in older people. They looked at the impact of forgiveness on 350 Spanish people 55 or older and found forgiveness showed significant positive impacts on both mental and physical health in older

---

2. *Book of Common Prayer*, p.3.
3. See page 28 through 30 of *The Forgiving Life* referenced earlier.
4. Lourdes Rey and Natalio Extremera, "Forgiveness and Health Related Quality of Life in Older People", *Journal of Health Psychology*

individuals. Other studies continue to demonstrate forgiveness is important for resilience, mental health, interpersonal connectedness, and overall flourishing. Charlotte vanOyen Witvliet and her colleagues had undergraduates imagine responding in a forgiving and unforgiving way to real-life offenders from their past. During these forgiving imagery exercises participants experienced immediate physiological benefits. They showed less physiological stress, lower levels of negative emotion, higher levels of positive emotion, and greater perceived control.[5] All of these positively impacted the well-being of the participants. In the same above mentioned book Enright discusses a study he and his group did with men dealing with coronary artery disease. In that study men who went through Enright's forgiveness process showed improved blood flow in their hearts and improved cardiac functionality. The fact that these men were able to forgive past hurt perpetrated on them led to a physiological change in how restricted their blood flow was to and through the heart. If what I propose is true regarding the holistic nature of being human and how the spiritual and emotional spheres impact all the others, then this makes perfect sense. We are not merely spiritual or emotional creatures nor are we merely physical creatures, we are holistically created creatures and healing in our emotions will demonstrate effects on our bodies.

Forgiveness is a powerful spiritual practice that positively impacts the manner in which we think about the world and other people, God, and ourselves. Forgiveness heals our emotional wounds and creates a more positive fulfilling sense of meaning and purpose in our lives. Forgiveness can heal our bodies and help them function better. It's a key factor to having healthy and fulfilling relationships and helps us be more like the God who created us. We must be icons of forgiveness in this broken world. We take on this vocation not just because it benefits us but because when we're healed and find ways to give and receive love, we initiate that same healing process in others.

---

5. Charlotte vanOyen Witvliet, Thomas E. Ludwig, and Kelly L. Vander "Granting Forgiveness or Harboring Grudges", *Psychological Science*

The Christian Vocation of Forgiveness

I read a book by Desmond Tutu called *No Future Without Forgiveness* in which he outlines how the new government of South Africa had to deal with all the pain, anger, and demands for justice erupting after Apartheid. At the end of the book he tells the story of how an Anglican nun, Sister Margaret Magdalen of the Community of St Mary the Virgin described the forgiving work of Jesus. Remember, Jesus dealt with plenty of hurt, pain, and rejection while ministering to others on earth. Desmund Tutu recalls Sister Mary explained Jesus dealt with all that garbage in the following way:

> She (Sister Mary) described it in terms of the difference between a vacuum cleaner and a dishwasher. The vacuum cleaner sucks up all the dirt and keeps it in the bag; whereas the dishwasher cleans up the dirty dishes and immediately spews forth all the filth into the drains. She contended that Jesus acted more like a dishwasher than a vacuum cleaner.[6]

Forgiveness is learning to be like a dishwasher and not a vacuum. Because we live in a broken world in which people hurt one another, we're going to get "dirty." Living in a world that doesn't understand we're meant to give and receive love means sometimes we're going to be hurt, angry and ashamed as well as broken and damaged. If we just suck that junk into our soul like a vacuum cleaner and never let go of what's lingering inside we'll die small deaths every day until we're emotionally dead long before our bodies fail us. We may be physically alive but we'll certainly be emotionally and spiritually dead. However, if we work through the pain just like a dishwasher by accepting it and then channeling it out of our emotional and spiritual lives in an appropriate way, we can live. We can live a truly flourishing life that gives hope and peace to a world expecting despair and pain. This is why we're called Christians; because we live lives that reflect Christ, the incarnate son of God who is the ultimate source of love, mercy, and forgiveness.

---

6. Desmund Tutu, *No Future Without Forgiveness*, 285

SUMMARY OF CHAPTER FIVE

This last chapter addressed the questions, "How can I be a forgiving person and what's the benefit of being one?" To be forgiving you have to do a few things. First, pray feverishly that God will reveal how much you're really hurting from what others have done to you and to be with you to comfort you as you explore that pain. Then, you have to develop some level of compassion and empathy for the person who hurt you. Once you do that you need to make the choice to forgive them and find ways to remind yourself you've extended that gift of forgiveness over and over again until you believe it yourself. If you get that far, you're on your way to finding peace and healing.

Because you choose to live a life of forgiveness you open the gateway to experiencing health in all the ways you are human. You receive physical benefits because of the reduced stress response anger and fear cause, you're able to think more clearly, emotionally open yourself up to love and be loved, enter into better relationships, and increase your sense of God in your life. Forgiveness may start with a cognitive choice but it benefits you physically, emotionally, spiritually, and relationally as well. Embrace this life not merely because of what it can do for you but because by doing so you are able to change the world so that one more human being has elected to be an agent of love and grace in the world instead of a perpetuator of fear, anger, brokenness, and hate.

Bibliography

"St. Teresa of Calcutta's Commencement Address to the Class of 1982," Thomas Aquinas College, accessed February 3, 2017, https://thomasaquinas.edu/about/light-new-light

Augustine. *Confessions*. Edited and translated by E. B. Pusey. London: Watkins, 2006.

Baron-Cohen, Simon. *The Science of Evil on Empathy and the Origins of Cruelty*. New York: Basic Books, 2011

Bonhoeffer, Dietrich. *Life Together, A Discussion of Christian Fellowship*. (New York: Harper & Row, 1954), 25—26

Book of Common Prayer (Cambridge: Cambridge University Press., 2011), p.3

C.S. Lewis *The Four Loves* (New York: Harcourt Brace & Company. 1960/1988), 39

Charlotte vanOyen Witvliet, Thomas E. Ludwig, and Kelly L. Vander "Granting Forgiveness or Harboring Grudges: Implications for Emotion, Physiology, and Health", *Psychological Science* 12, no. 2 (2001)

Desmund Tutu, *No Future Without Forgiveness* (New York: Doubleday, 1999), 285

Everett J. Worthington Jr., "The Pyramid Model of Forgiveness," in *Dimensions of Forgiveness, Psychological Research & Theological Perspectives*, ed. Everett J. Worthington Jr. (Radnor PA: Templeton Foundation Press, 1998), 119.

Lois Lowry, *The Giver* (New York: Houghton Mifflin, 1993), 103

Lourdes Rey and Natalio Extremera, "Forgiveness and Health Related Quality of Life in Older People: Adaptive Cognitive Emotion Regulation Strategies as Mediators", *Journal of Health Psychology* 21, no.12 (2016)

Robert D. Enright, *The Forgiving Life: A Pathway to Overcoming Resentment and Creating a Legacy of Love* (Washington DC: American Psychological Association, 2012), 168.

Bibliography

The Ante-Nicene Fathers. Edited by Alexander Roberts and James Donaldson. 1885–1887. 10 vols. Repr., Peabody, MA: Hendrickson, 1994.

Tullian Tchividjian, "Trouble Happens," in *The Road We Must Travel*, (Brentwood TN: Worthy Publishing, 2014), Kindle edition.

William Flack Jr., James D. Laird, and Lorraine A. Cavallaro. "Separate and Combined Effects of Facial Expressions and Bodily Postures on Emotional Feelings" *European Journal of Social Psychology*, 29 (1999)

www.ingramcontent.com/pod-product-compliance
Lightning Source LLC
Chambersburg PA
CBHW070920160426
43193CB00011B/1542